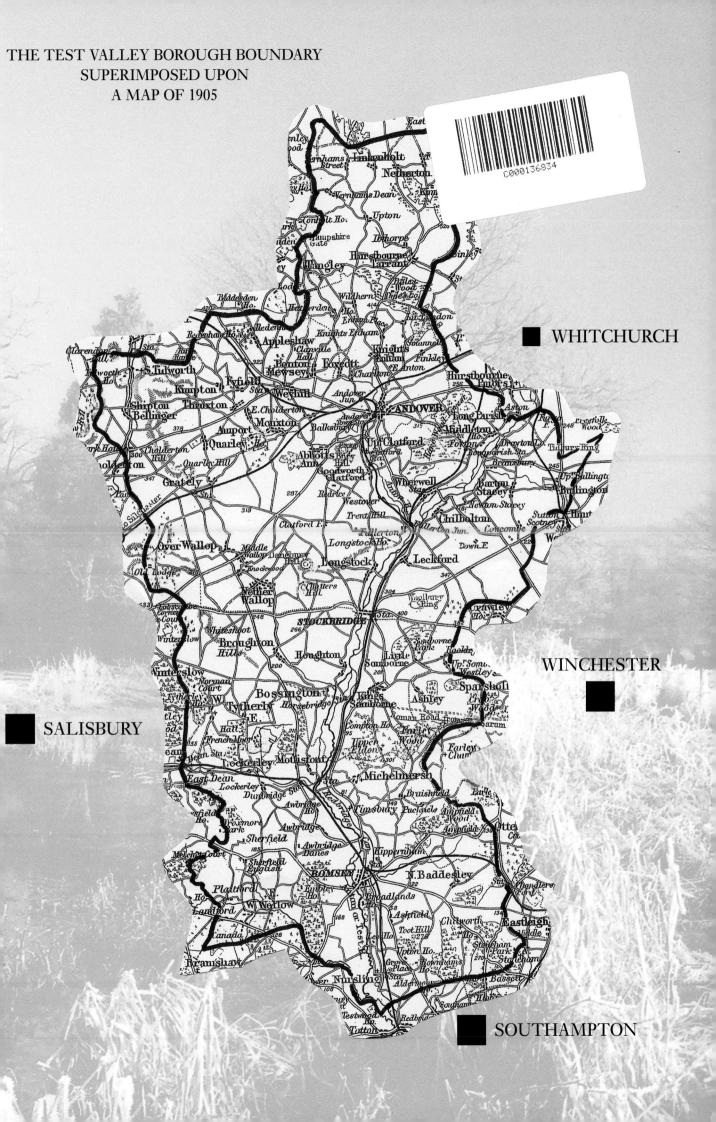

THE
CHURCHES
OF TEST VALLEY

BY

BRYAN AND DIANA BEGGS

'A photographic and historical odyssey'

SECOND EDITION 2010

SOLD IN AID OF TEST VALLEY ARTS FOUNDATION

Test Valley Arts Foundation is an independent grant making charity established in 1991 by the late Michael Colvin MP. Its key objectives are to encourage a wide range of arts and music in Test Valley by supporting cultural activity and helping talented individuals and groups to develop their work.

Since its inception the Foundation has made grants amounting to £75,000.

PUBLISHED BY
TEST VALLEY CHURCHES BOOK SOCIETY
27 The Avenue
Andover
Hampshire SP10 3EP

PRINTED AND BOUND BY
ADVENT COLOUR
19 East Portway
Andover
Hampshire SP10 3LU

ISBN 978-0-9556631-4-7

✧ ✧ ✧

The authors wish to acknowledge the kind permission of the following publishers and copyright holders, for the ability to include certain quotations in this book.
RANDOM HOUSE for extracts from The Complete Poems by C.Day. Lewis published by Sinclair-Stevenson [1992] Copyright 1992 in this edition The Estate of C. Day. Lewis.
THE ESTATE OF MURIEL STUART [Mrs. Stapleforth]
FABER and FABER for the quotation from W.H.Auden's, 'O love the interest itself'.
THE LITERARY TRUSTEES of Walter De La Mare and THE SOCIETY OF AUTHORS as their representative, for the extract from 'Frescoes in an Old Church'.
JOHN MURRAY [Publishers] Ltd for extracts from 'Hymn' and 'Church of England Thoughts', in 'Collected Poems' by Sir John Betjeman.
DAVID HIGHAM Associates, for the extracts from 'Set in a Silver Sea' by Sir Arthur Bryant; published by Book Club Associates [by arrangement with William Collins Sons & Co Ltd.]

For the few other quotations, which may be within copyright; we regret to say that our efforts to locate the authors, sources and copyright holders have been unsuccessful, for which we apologise.

✧ ✧ ✧

BIBLIOGRAPHY

Victoria County History of Hampshire.
Hampshire .... J. Charles Cox F.S.A.
Churches Conservation Trust .... Booklets for Little Somborne, Upper Eldon and Ashley.
Abbotts Ann .... Mrs. Pamela King.
Ampfield .... Hallett and Wood.
St. Mary's Church Andover .... Arthur Bennett.
A Pioneer in Xanadu [Denys Rolle 1725-1797] .... Rev'd. Robert Legg
Broughton in Hampshire ....Robert Parr and Baron Sewter.
Shipton Bellinger, 'The story of a village' ....J.Hinde, S.Hart and T.Kaye.
Wherwell... History and Legend ......'J.R.D.' [1990], based upon Anthony Tuke [1975].
Aspects of Wherwell Abbey .... Kate Clark.
Mottisfont Abbey .... National Trust Guide Book.
Lookback No. 3 ..... [Official Journal] Andover Local History Society.
The Church by The Arch .... Ian Stirling.
Romsey Baptist Church .... Rev'd. F.M.Perkins and R.J.Higgins.
The Catholic Church, Romsey .... Fr. Louis Catterall, SMM.
North Baddesley Church and Village .... K.J.Ritchie, M.A., F.S.A.
Charlton. History of the Church of St. Thomas ....Gerald Gould.
Romsey Abbey .... The Pitkin Guide.
Hampshire Nunneries .... Diana Coldicott.
Andover. A Pictorial History .... Derek J. Tempero.

CONTENTS

TO
DUNCAN

Even the youths shall faint and be weary
and the young men shall utterly fall,
but they that wait upon the Lord,
shall renew their strength,
they shall mount up with wings as eagles
they shall run and not be weary
they shall walk and not faint.

ISAIAH Chap 40 vv 30-31.

THE ABOVE VERSES ARE PART OF THE DESIGN
OF THE NEW EAST WINDOW TO HIS MEMORY
IN ST. MICHAEL AND ALL ANGELS CHURCH, ANDOVER

OUR PERSONAL ACKNOWLEDGEMENTS

RELATING TO THIS EDITION

Mr. David Gleave   Economic Development Officer Test Valley Borough Council. A facilitator "par excellence" and a valued adviser at all times.

✧ ✧ ✧

Mr. Andrew Bateman   Tourism Manager [H.C.C.] For his support of this project.

✧ ✧ ✧

The following County Councillors, who responded so generously under the terms of the Hampshire County Councillors' 'Devolved Budget Scheme'.

County Councillor Mark Cooper
County Councillor David Drew
County Councillor Mrs. Pamela Mutton
County Councillor Roy Perry

✧ ✧ ✧

Honorary Alderman [H.C.C.] George. W. Porter   A most loyal and respected friend and supporter of this project.

✧ ✧ ✧

The Chairman and Committee of 'Hampshire and the Islands Historic Churches Trust' for their keen interest and support.

✧ ✧ ✧

Mr. David Holdaway   For his specialist advice and typesetting skills, once again.

Mr. Adam De Marco   and his design team at Advent Colour.

AUTHORS' TRIBUTE TO FIRST EDITION SPONSORS

The first edition of this book would never have been printed without the generosity of family members, who opted to record the names of their deceased relations in the IN MEMORIAM section of that book. We remain indebted to them for their commitment to our endeavour. The full list of those original names is remembered below.

ALLMARK Edward [Ted]
ALMOND Cecilia
ARCHER Ethel [Ettie]
ARCHER Frank Albert
BABEY Cyril Robert
BAKER Dorothy Aileen
BEAVES Florence Elizabeth
BEAVES Fred
BEGGS David Arthur
BEGGS Kathleen Lucy
BEGGS Duncan Bryan
BENNETT Edward Goodwin
BENNETT Marjorie
BERRY Cyril John James
BLACKWOOD Edward James.
BLOOMFIELD Elsie Grace
BLOOMFIELD Jesse Augustus
BLYTHE Kathleen H.
BOYES Hazel E.
BRAND Arthur W. C.
BRAND Muriel A.
BROOKS Peter
CABLE Ralph Gardiner
CABLE Winifred Amy
CHAMBERS Bridget
CHAMBERS Rev'd. John Gilbert
CHERRY Arthur William
COLEBROOK Rev'd. Canon John Ridley
COLVIN Michael Keith Beale M.P.
COLVIN The Hon. Nichola
COOKE Andrew John Campbell
COOPER Blanche Beatrice
COOPER Leonard William
CORNICK Patricia May
DAVIES Beryl Iris
DAVIES H.J. [Bobby]
DAVIES Malcolm J. G. LRAM ARCM
DAVIES Iris Eileen
DAVIES Wilfred John
DENNIS John Frank
DENTON Dorothy May
DENTON Felicity Anne Franchesca
DENTON Lynn Christine B.Sc.Hons.
DENTON Valerie Frances May
DENTON William George
DENTON Marjorie Grace
DOUGLAS Frederick Walter D.F.M.
DUTT Anup K.
EAGAR Edward Desmond Russell
EARLE Donovan Hayes
EARLE Margaret Fanny
ELLIOTT Joy Amelia

EXALL Rev'd. John A. B.Sc.
FAHY Adrian Francis
FENN Ernest Anthony Robin [Tony]
FISK Constance Christina
FRANCIS Barbara Joan
GALLOP Kenneth Anthony [Tony]
GASKELL Alan
GILBERT Gladys Emily
GILLESPIE Lt. Col. Rollo F. F. O.B.E.
GILLESPIE Daphne Helen
GOTHARD Alan Sidney
GRIFFITHS Betty
GROVER Lt. Col. David L. M.
HARDING Brian Frank
HARDING Frank Robert
HARDY Olave Mary
HARDY Reginald
HARRIS Edward Albert
HARRIS Muriel Winifred
HARRISON Reginald Stanhope
HERRIDGE Dorothy
HERRIDGE Charles Edward
HILL Lawrence Jeffrey
HITCHCOCK Walter
HUMPHRIES Winifred [Helen]
HUNT Charles Stanbrook [Stan]
HUNT Janet
HURD Avril
INGLIS Alan Meredith
INGS Christopher Victor D.S.M.
JENKINS Don
JOHNS Edwin
JOURNEAUX Barbara Eileen
LAKE Joan
LANGDON Graham Stanley
LATREILLE Elizabeth Ann
LATTER Lesley Alfred
LOWMAN Joyce Philippa
MACHELL Eric Samuel B.Sc., FSARCS
MANSBRIDGE Dorothy
MANSBRIDGE Pamela Louise
MARTELL George William D.S.M.
MASTERS Susannah
McCALLUM Donald
MOLE Gordon Edward
MOORE Alice Georgina
MOORE John Charles
MORGAN John L.
MORRELL Frank
MORRELL Gertrude Mary
MOULAND John [Jack]
MURRAY Maggie Ann

NEWBURY Richard Norman
NEWMAN Lena
NEWNHAM Philippa Mary
NORRIS Frederick John
OLIVER Charles
OLIVER Margaret Elizabeth
PAUFFLEY Eric John
PAUFFLEY Lucy Anne
PENTON Ivy
PENTON Percy Lesley
PERKINS Edith Mary
PERRY Alan Charles
PERRY Dora Emily
PETTET Arthur William
PETTET Peggy
RANDALL Harry Thomas
RAWLINGS Donald
RAWLINGS Doodie
RAYER Edward Kenneth Westbury
RAYNOR Margaret Mavis
ROSS Margaret Joan
SEAGER Margaret
SHEPPARD Irene
SIMPSON Frank Roby
SLOAN Lesley Catherine
SPURGEON Sqn. Ldr. Charles Ernest
SPURGEON Jean
STAFFORD Belinda Jane
STORER Anthony Hugh [Tony]
STUBINGS Charles Albert
STUBINGS Alice Theodora
SUTTON Samantha Jane
TARRANT James [Jim]
TARRANT Molly
TILLEY Molly B.
TRASLER Doris E.
TROLLOPE Ronald Elwyn
TUKE Sir Anthony Favill Kt.
TUKE Anthony William
WALKER Charles Ninian
WALKER Norah May
WALKER Norman Mackie
WEEKS Stuart John
WHEELER Clifford Albert
WHITE Dr. John Edward FRCP
WILSON John C. G. MBE
WOOD Arthur James
WOOD Lilian Esther
WOOD Eustace William
WOOD Margaret Ivy LRAM
WOOD M. Eileen

A PRAYER

Gracious God and Heavenly Father, help us as we each make our own way to the foot of Your Cross.
Help us to leave with You there, our burdens of pain, anxiety, resentfulness or loss;
then to walk ever onwards in Your strength, and the light of Your enduring love,
until we attain perfect healing and wholeness with You forever. Amen

FOREWORD

The Bishop of Winchester
The Rt Revd Michael Scott-Joynt

The Diocese of
Winchester

THE CHURCH
OF ENGLAND

The Diocese of Winchester was founded in 676 AD. Today it covers a large part of Hampshire as well as Bournemouth and the Channel Islands.

In our country we are blessed with a rich heritage of churches of all denominations bearing witness to faithful worship and Christian discipleship throughout many centuries, and the Test Valley – one of the most beautiful parts of Hampshire – is full of these gems, each with its own story to tell, as you will find in the pages of this book.

I had the pleasure of opening, together with the Mayor of the Test Valley, the author's Millennium Exhibition of these photographs in Andover Museum in September 2000. In 2005, when launching the first edition of this book, I much welcomed it as a means of re-acquainting myself with the collection. I was confident then that it would prove an inspiring guide, freshly illuminating some of the familiar buildings of the Borough area, as well as introducing the reader to some much less obvious, yet still very precious, places of worship. I am pleased to learn that, all first edition copies having been sold, £1500 has been donated to both The Countess of Brecknock Hospice in Andover, and to Countess Mountbatten House in Southampton.

Likewise, I am delighted now to associate myself with the aims of this second edition, which I see is to be sold in aid of the Test Valley Arts Foundation, and which I hope will encourage residents and visitors alike to appreciate the local heritage in its unique Test Valley setting.

+Michael Winton
October 2010

TEST VALLEY – AN HISTORICAL PERSPECTIVE

Probably one of the oldest settlements within Test Valley and barely 15 miles from Stonehenge, Andover developed as a town in the 10th Century because there was easy access to the river, and on the higher ground, the people could be protected from the occasional flooding of the river valley.

It is known that people were of course living in the area some 2000 years earlier. Just beyond the present confines of Harewood Forest, on what was once Chilbolton airfield, some burial mounds of the "Stonehenge period" have revealed finds of great significance... namely the "hair ornaments or ear adornments", of pure Irish gold and the blade of a copper dagger of Spanish origin. [These finds are exhibited in the Andover Museum.] This museum, in Church Close, was once the home of Mrs. Poore, whom Jane Austen visited in 1800. There is also access to the Museum of the Iron Age in the adjoining building, where finds from the excavations at nearby Danebury Hill between 1969 and 1983 [carried out by Professor Sir Barry Cunliffe C.B.E.] are on display.

Of course the Romans left their mark on Test Valley with the Portway and the Icknield Way roads crossing just to the east of Andover, some notable villas and a newly discovered water mill at Fullerton. The more important Test Valley finds are in the British Museum [e.g. The Appleshaw Hoard]. A nearly complete Roman mosaic floor of impressive size has recently been mounted for display, inside the entrance to the Iron Age Museum.

The "blossoming" of Christian institutions during the Saxon period, in particular the abbeys at Romsey and Nursling and the important connection of the latter with the evangelism of St Boniface in present day Germany and The Netherlands, was followed later by their devastation by the Vikings. These events are all part of our rich heritage... as was the eventual conversion of the Vikings to Christianity, resulting from St. Olaf's personal conversion and confirmation in Andover in AD 994.

As England became established by King Alfred the Great and his descendants and later Norman kings, Romsey Abbey was rebuilt at least twice. At the other end of the "scale" tiny local Saxon churches also built of stone, began to appear, replacing those of wattle, daub and thatch. Unsurprisingly, even these have long since disappeared or been "adapted" to suit later generations... the existing church at Little Somborne is probably the most original. Although Winchester was the Saxon capital of England it was the practice for the "seat of government" to be where the king was at any particular time, hence the royal "councils" which are recorded in Grateley and Knights Enham, and in Andover itself. One of these monarchs, Edgar, was reported to have slain his friend Earl Athelwold in Harewood Forest... a cross [illustrated opposite] was placed in the woodland in the 19th Century to commemorate the occurrence by the landowner.

Many of our churches survive from the time of the Normans and their medieval successor kings, from the notable and majestic rebuilt Romsey Abbey to the tiniest one of all at Ashley. We hope you will discover your own favourites from within the pages of this book and go on to experience at first hand their sanctity and calm.

The "new learning" of the 16th Century protestant Reformation created other tensions; Mottisfont Abbey was rebuilt as a private house, but Wherwell Abbey was "dissolved" by Henry VIII and then demolished. Romsey Abbey was purchased by the inhabitants of the town.

In the Civil War of the 17th Century, minor battles and skirmishes took place in this area at Abbotts Ann and Penton, and the opposing armies marched through... King Charles stayed at the Angel in Andover on his way to the Second Battle of Newbury.

Largely lacking the natural resources which were vital to the Industrial Revolution of the 18th and 19th Centuries, Hampshire in general and Test Valley in particular were not greatly affected by it, but the "Waterloo Ironworks" of the Tasker family at Anna Valley and the development of the brewing industry in Romsey, both achieved national importance.

The expansion of non-conformism in the 19th Century saw the erection of chapels in our villages... many are still in use. The Church of England saw a revival too, and it was betweem 1840 and 1846 that the Norman church of St. Mary in Andover was replaced by the fine example of Victorian church architecture, with its beautiful stained glass windows, that we see today standing proudly above the town.

In the 20th Century Test Valley was transformed for the purposes of two World Wars with the provision and enlargement of Army camps, and airfields for the R.A.F., of which Middle Wallop [now the home of the Army Air Corps] is the most historic. Here is where the Museum of Army Flying records this history, together with that of more recent conflicts of the 20th and 21st Centuries, in an interesting and dramatic way.

TEST VALLEY – TIMELINE

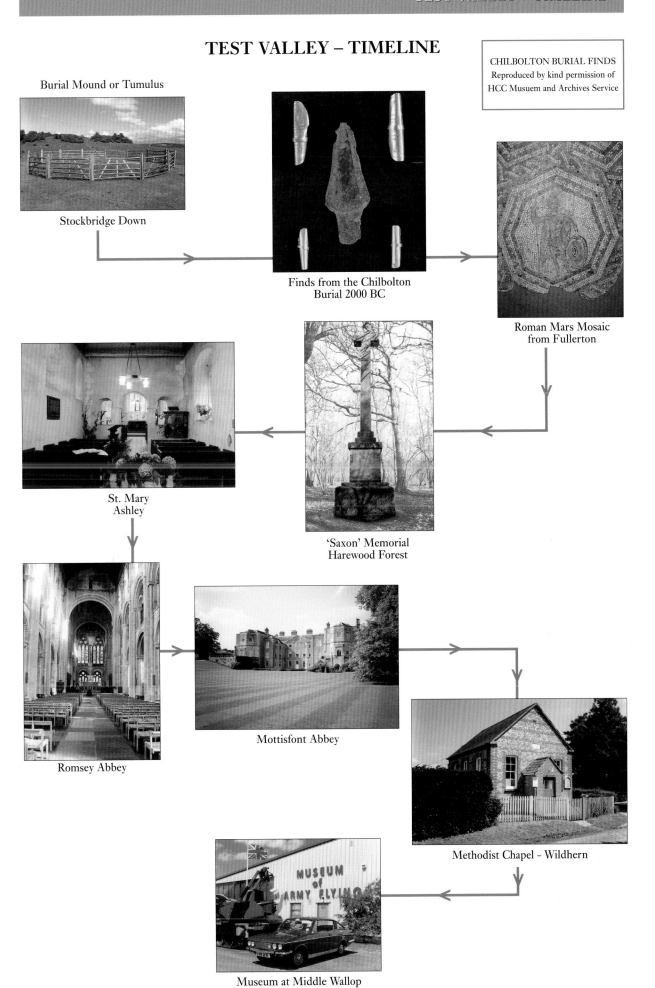

CHILBOLTON BURIAL FINDS
Reproduced by kind permission of
HCC Musuem and Archives Service

Burial Mound or Tumulus

Stockbridge Down

Finds from the Chilbolton
Burial 2000 BC

Roman Mars Mosaic
from Fullerton

St. Mary
Ashley

'Saxon' Memorial
Harewood Forest

Romsey Abbey

Mottisfont Abbey

Methodist Chapel - Wildhern

Museum at Middle Wallop

TOWNS OF TEST VALLEY

The quotes in italics are from *Highways and Byways in Hampshire* by D.H. Moutray Read, dated 1908.

"The stranger who has wandered around Andover ignorant of its history would probably judge the town to date no further back than, at most, the day of stage coaches, or maybe from the coming of the railway..., but Andover is old. Very very *old. Back into the dim ages when Neolithic man lorded it over the stretching Downs, still dotted with his memorials, even before history has a word to say... this town that appears so essentially modern, may claim its origin."*

ANDOVER...
A modern market town

The High Street of Andover is dominated by its Guildhall and the Victorian church of St. Mary's, known as the "Cathedral of north-west Hampshire". The church is built above the ruins of an original Norman church, on the

hill around which the town began in Saxon times, or earlier [see above]. Some 15th Century houses still exist in this area [e.g. THE ANGEL Inn] but most of the remaining historic buildings are of the prosperous 18th Century when the town was an important stopping point for stagecoaches on their way from London to the West Country. The story of Andover's history is told in the Andover Museum in Church Close, which also gives access to the Museum of the Iron Age and the Tourist Information Centre. Through this very door, came Jane Austen to visit her friend Mrs. Poore in November 1800.

Do wander around the attractive High St. [markets on Thursday and Saturday] and the narrow walkways leading from it, where you will discover smaller shops and antique galleries and the town's modern indoor CHANTRY WAY shopping complex.

THE LIGHTS, Andover's professional arts and entertainment venue, close by on the Andover College campus, is the hub of creative activity for this part of the county.

✧ ✧ ✧

"The way to come to Romsey is from Salisbury... from the hill above the broad Test valley, the abbey church stands out impressively, dwarfing the buildings of the modern town especially when the sun is low enough to leave Romsey in shadow, that tones down the rows of brick and slate to a mere suggestion of red and grey amongst the trees, above the thread of the river, which holds the changing colours of the sky prisoned below in the flat meadows, before it passes under Middlebridge to wash the grassy lawns of Broadlands."

ROMSEY...
Community and Tradition

This small market town on the banks of the River Test is a fascinating place to explore either before or after a visit to BROADLANDS, the Palladian style home of the late Lord Mountbatten, with its connections to royalty.

On Romsey's winding streets, medieval gems such as KING JOHN'S LODGE rub shoulders with 18th and 19th Century civic buildings that reflect the town's days as a thriving brewing and market centre.

Watching over all is the impressive ROMSEY ABBEY built in Norman times and little altered since those days. If you visit in July there is the Beggars Fair, and throughout the summer months the area around the Corn Exchange buzzes with street entertainers. A lively market takes place on Tuesdays and Fridays. September is the month of the famous Romsey Show in the grounds of the Broadlands estate.

Nearby, East Wellow is a famous place on the "tourist trail". In the churchyard of the beautiful 13th Century church, which is dedicated to St. Margaret, is the dignified monument to the first lady ever to have been awarded the Order of Merit, FLORENCE NIGHTINGALE. The wording on her tomb simply reads "F.N. Born 15th May 1820. Died 13th August 1910".

✧ ✧ ✧

"Though summer droughts had stolen the colours from the Downs... purple shadows broke and gathered on the blue hills. Even the bare earth in fields lying fallow had warmth in its pale reds, and the broken chalk cliffs on the eastern side of the valley glowed dazzlingly white above the lush-grass of the river levels. The Test glinted with the blue of polished steel through the tangle of water plants and rushes.... Coming from the Downs with their sunburnt grasses, the vivid display and contrast was a sight to remember. This one thought, must be Stockbridge at its best."

STOCKBRIDGE...
History and Character

Lying at the heart of Test Valley, there are many reasons to visit Stockbridge. The unusually wide High Street reflects its earlier role as a drovers road, but this charming small town is now less of a staging post and more famous as England's fly-fishing "capital".

The main course of the River Test flows under a bridge at the west end of the street, but its many subsidiary streamlets flow between the shops and houses, and beside footpaths. Rights to the fishing on this part of the Test belong to the exclusive Houghton Fishing Club, founded in 1822, which has its meeting room over the entrance of the town's GROSVENOR HOTEL.

This is a place to take time to browse the galleries and antique shops and to take refreshment in one of the many teashops, restaurants and pubs, or stroll across the common beside the river and perhaps see the trout or even a kingfisher!

The TEST WAY FOOTPATH passes through the town along the line of a former railway; this fact alone makes the town an ideal base from which to experience the variety of country walks available... not forgetting the views from the National Trust open area of Stockbridge Down.

TRIBUTES

From County Councillor Roy Perry
Deputy Leader, Hampshire County Council

As chairman of Test Valley Arts Foundation, I welcome the 2nd edition of this delightful photographic record of the churches of Test Valley and congratulate Bryan and Diana Beggs for their own artistic achievement in producing this wonderful photographic record.

The book is a work of art in itself and an amazing testament, not just to the expressions of faith in this part of Hampshire for over 1000 years but also a reminder that art and beauty have been created over those years, in and through the beautiful places of worship recorded in this book.

I welcome this opportunity to say how grateful the Test Valley Arts Foundation is to be the recipient of the proceeds from the sales of this book. Throughout history artists have always needed patrons and we seek to help the artists of the 21st century to develop their work for the benefit of future generations. May their work too survive for a 1000 years just like the Mediaeval Wall Paintings to be found in some churches.

✧ ✧ ✧

From Roger Tetstall
Chief Executive, Test Valley Borough Council

I am so pleased to be able to lend the support of the Borough Council to this lovely second edition. I wholeheartedly support its aim of attracting visitors, and encouraging residents, to enjoy the beautiful heritage of the Test Valley. I believe that our wonderful array of parish churches bears comparison with anywhere in the British Isles. They add greatly to the charm and character of our settlements, together with the surrounding countryside and other historic features and buildings. Alongside our local fare and produce, these are the elements that make up the distinctive character that is 'Test Valley' and which is so valuable to our local economy.

✧ ✧ ✧

From Andrew Bateman
Tourism Manager, Hampshire County Council

Hampshire is one of the largest and oldest of English counties, lying at the heart of central southern England. Its landscape and architecture, its folklore, history, food, drink all help to define Hampshire's rich heritage – and to make it unique. These assets have also enabled Hampshire to develop a vibrant tourism industry contributing an estimated £2.7 billion to the Hampshire economy and supporting over 65,000 jobs.

Hampshire's rich array of village churches play an important part in the county's tourism offer and by encouraging church tourism we can help increase their ability to generate income to support their fabric, and help our visitors to be more aware of their historical and artistic importance.

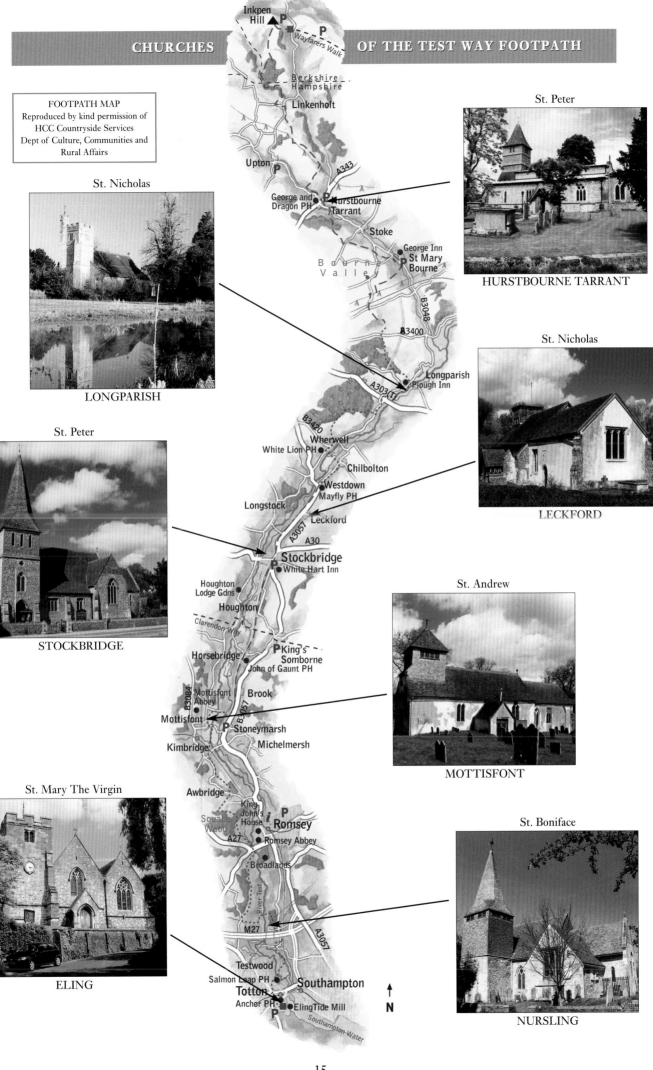

FOOTPATH MAP
Reproduced by kind permission of
HCC Countryside Services
Dept of Culture, Communities and
Rural Affairs

St. Peter

HURSTBOURNE TARRANT

St. Nicholas

LONGPARISH

St. Nicholas

LECKFORD

St. Peter

STOCKBRIDGE

St. Andrew

MOTTISFONT

St. Mary The Virgin

ELING

St. Boniface

NURSLING

15

CHAIRMAN'S LETTER

I am delighted to have this opportunity to associate the work of our County Trust with this second edition of Bryan and Diana Beggs' successful book 'The Churches of Test Valley'. It was a great pleasure to be presented with the last copy of the first edition of this book when I was invited to launch the Test Valley Borough Council's pamphlet 'Parish Churches of Test Valley', last June.

The Trust, which is a charity, was formed in 1988 and raises funds to repair and improve the fabric and contents of Churches of all denominations which are of historic or architectural interest, as well as to their surrounding churchyards. Since our foundation we have raised and made grants totalling over £700,000 to deserving cases throughout our area of responsibility, which as our title implies, includes the Isle of Wight and the Channel Islands.

The predominant source of our revenue comes from the organisation of our 'Ride and Stride' event, which is held every year on the second Saturday in September, when we invite anyone to seek sponsorship and visit as many churches as possible during the day, cycling or walking from one to the other. Individual churches will often provide our volunteers with suitable refreshments and it makes a wonderful family outing... choosing your own route means you can avoid the hills if you wish!

During 2009, two of the nine churches to which we made grants, were in Test Valley... the charming little church of St. James, Bossington, which is a little off the beaten track and all that remains of a 'lost' village, and St Mary Broughton, a fine example of a traditional parish church right in the centre of a very thriving community... both of course feature in this volume.

There are over forty photographs of places where our grants have 'made a difference', on our website ' hampshirehistoricchurches.org.uk', which readers of this book may care to access online, where full details of our work can be found. We should of course, be delighted if such readers would like to become members of the Trust and thereby increase our ability to help those who apply for our aid. For those without access to the internet, our Hon Sec. can be contacted, c/o Hampshire Record Office, Sussex Street, Winchester. SO23 8TH

Joan E. Appleyard

28. 10. 10

INTRODUCTION TO THE SECOND EDITION

Our ability to publish this new edition, with its first section now revised to emphasise the role that our heritage plays in welcoming tourists to this beautiful part of Hampshire, derives mainly from the interest and support of the Test Valley Borough Council and certain Hampshire County Councillors, who represent our area.

Other departments of the County Council and personal friends have played their part too… formal acknowledgement of their contributions is made elsewhere. We might say this volume has been a "community effort" and we are very grateful to everyone.

The first edition was published in 2005 and evolved as a response to some of the generous comments made by many persons, who visited the Millennium Exhibition in Andover Museum entitled "All The Churches of Test Valley", which we had photographed over the previous six years.

Our exhibition of over seventy photographs was presented again the following year in Romsey Abbey, and was seen by an estimated 8000 visitors. Both exhibitions were made possible only through the generous help of the Hampshire County Museum Service and Test Valley Borough Council.

As was always the intention, when the exhibition finally closed, all the framed photographs were passed to the individual churches for safe-keeping; they have since found a home either in the churches themselves, or church halls, village halls, schools or vicarages.

As Bryan began to write the text for the book, we realised that it was not just the churches he was writing about, but the whole history of the borough. At our every entry through this porch or that lych-gate, our history was all around us, tangible and enfolding. Not only did each one have its own story to tell, but soon they all began to fit together like a great jig-saw puzzle to produce a coherent whole, a tapestry of life and experience, of art and architecture, of which all of us are the inheritors and to which we are still contributors.

It would be impossible for us to list all those individuals [as often as not, churchwardens], who on receipt of an enquiry "out of the blue", offered to meet, conduct and instruct us during our travels. Sometimes Bryan intruded unwittingly, for example, upon organists and flower-arrangers and yet such was

their care and concern for their church, that they gave willingly of their time to answer his questions and show him the "gems" of their particular church. Throughout our researches we tried to avoid "bothering" incumbents, but when there was no alternative, we received from them most helpful advice, and the names of useful contacts, which often opened up new areas of research and information.

Furthermore, we wish to record our indebtedness to all those kind and industrious persons, mostly anonymous, who have produced and updated the individual booklets and pamphlets that are available in almost all of our churches in Test Valley, and from which facts and inspiration have been drawn. In some cases a more detailed history of a church and/or a town or village is available in a separate publication, and these are listed elsewhere as are the other reference volumes we have consulted.

As in the first edition we are delighted to be able to include as a frontispiece, our photograph which we call "The Shadow of the Cross" taken in Tangley church on 5th July 1994. As Bryan noted when we first received the print after the film was developed…
The presence in this print of a shadow of a cross just below the point of the chancel arch outlined with blocks of pale purple light is inexplicable. It was not visible to me at the time, and is not the result of anything that I tried to do. There is no window or reflective surface that could in any way have caused this light to appear in the form it had taken… we found it very inspirational.

It is our duty to record also that the first edition was financed by advance subscriptions from the families and friends of those whose names appeared in a detailed "In Memoriam" section of the book. The list on page 8 reminds us of them and provides a link with the past.

Finally, we would again ask our readers to note that this book was never intended to be a "scholarly tome", for neither of us have architectural or historical qualifications, it merely reflects our desire to share our interest in a vital aspect of local history. We shall consider our endeavours a success, if any readers are encouraged to share our experiences by visiting these inspiring buildings and seeing their contents for themselves. They are the inheritance of us all, bequeathed to us by the former inhabitants of the places, in which we have the good fortune to dwell.

St Thomas of Canterbury, Tangley
Noon, 5th July 1994.

Hold Thou Thy Cross before my closing eyes;
Shine through the gloom, and point me to the skies;
Heaven's morning breaks, and earth's vain shadows flee;
In life, in death, O Lord, abide with me.

THE
CHURCHES
OF TEST VALLEY

PLEASE NOTE
THAT
FOR EASE OF REFERENCE
THE CHURCHES ARE PRESENTED
IN
ALPHABETICAL ORDER

ABBOTTS ANN
St. Mary the Virgin

That time of year thou mayst in me behold
When yellow leaves, or none, or few, do hang
Upon those boughs which shake against the cold,
Bare ruined choirs, where late the sweet birds sang.

WILLIAM SHAKESPEARE 1564 - 1616

William Shakespeare died exactly one hundred years before this church was rebuilt in the new Classical style, on the same site as its predecessor, which one suspects might have been in great need of repair, though the *ruined choirs* of Shakespeare's sonnet of course refer to the trees of autumn. Never-the-less, in the upper photograph taken on the 7th October 1997, we hope you may notice the *yellow leaves... shake against the cold* of an early morning.

This church, dedicated to St. Mary the Virgin was built by Thomas Pitt in 1716. He was the grandfather of one of our greatest prime ministers and great-grandfather of a second. In 1715 he was appointed a 'Parliamentary Commissioner for New Churches', and having bought the manor of Abbotts Ann from William Blake of Andover in 1710, he obviously decided to lead by example on his own estate. This church cost precisely £1,197 and sixpence halfpenny, and the work was supervised by his son Robert. It was Robert, who aged just 21 in 1702, had carried secretly to England from India, the largest diamond ever discovered up to that time in the whole world, which his father when Governor of Madras, had privately purchased. No wonder Thomas Pitt was known as 'Diamond' Pitt! He eventually sold the cut diamond weighing 136 carats to the French Government in 1717. It was in fact bought by the Regent of France on behalf of the five year old King Louis XV for £135,000... the equivalent today would be about £9 million. It has been known as The Regent Diamond ever since and survived the French Revolution, theft, and two World Wars, and is today on display in the Louvre Museum in Paris.

We are fortunate indeed to have several churches in Test Valley which are 'of their time' with few if any alterations... this is one of them. We believe we may safely assume that Commissioner Pitt sought guidance from the famous Surveyor General, Sir Christopher Wren, in designing this church but there is no proof. It is an excellent example of its period but we can only surmise what the initial reaction might have been in the locality, when this brick building enlivened with the whiteness of the Portland stone pilasters, replaced something perhaps of flint and chalk with probably a thatched roof. The light flooding in from the huge Georgian windows alone, would have been a complete contrast to whatever had been there before. The interior is one to relish for it still has a western gallery supported on magnificent oak Tuscan columns, and its box pews, pulpit, altar table and font are almost exactly as they were in 1716. The only additions are the Victorian stained glass in some windows in the chancel, and the organ which was installed in 1888.

The interior also bears witness to the fact that this parish shares with only two others in England, [Ashford-in-the-Water, Derbyshire, and Minsterley, Shropshire] the distinction of maintaining the tradition of 'the virgin crowns'. Apparently this tradition was quite widespread during the time of Queen Elizabeth I [The Virgin Queen]. It was certainly known to Shakespeare for in Hamlet he has a priest at Ophelia's burial say, "...Yet here she is allowed her virgin crants" [meaning crown, from 'krantz', the German for a wreath or garland]. A virgin crown can be requested by the family of a deceased person, but may only be awarded on behalf of someone who was born, baptised, confirmed <u>and</u> died unmarried in the parish. The full explanation is given in the informative pamphlet available to visitors inside the church. This also draws attention to the wonderful embroidery on the kneelers and cushions in the church, forty-nine of which record the names of recipients of the crowns, and are a modern enhancement to its heritage. The very appropriate quotation on the kneelers at the sanctuary rail, is taken from verse 10 of the second chapter of St. Paul's Epistle to the Philippians... 'at the name of Jesus every knee should bow'.

AMPFIELD
St. Mark

The western sky is glowing yet... The burnish'd cross upon the spire
Gives token where the sun has set, Touch'd faintly with its last dim fire.

Lyra Innocentium. JOHN KEBLE 1792 - 1866

Rev'd. John Keble, an accomplished poet as well as priest, may well have had the steeple of St. Mark's in his mind when composing the lines above, certainly this church will forever be associated with him, he being one of the three main leaders of The Oxford Movement. This was a 19th century reformation in thinking about the meaning and form of services in the Church of England. It advocated a return to a more spiritual and mystical experience.

Keble had been the tutor at Oxford of Sir William Heathcote of Hursley Park, who persuaded him to come to Hursley as incumbent in 1836. Here under the protection of his patron, he was able to continue to influence the church. Much emphasis was placed upon the restoration and beautification of churches in general. St. Mark's was built entirely at Sir William's expense between September 1838 and April 1841 and was greatly needed... Hursley parish at that time being an area of widely scattered communities.

The architect of St. Mark's was Mr.O.Carter of Winchester; it is said that his designs for the east and west windows [by William Wailes], were inspired by his knowledge of windows in Lincoln Cathedral and Beverley Minster respectively. The east window was the gift of Rev'd. R.F. Wilson [the first vicar here], who later became Vicar of Rownhams. The church's design incorporated a north gallery, now adapted to provide space for the organ and access to a fine modern extension. Inside the nave all the wood is dark and richly carved, pews, pulpit, lectern etc. A smart modern carpet in green and purple runs the length of the aisle. The purple shade is picked up in the curtain over the south door, and the green, in the eleven Gothic arches behind the altar, where there is a special shelf for the large brass cross, enriched with semi-precious stones.

In Ampfield, we are in "rhododendron-land" and visitors in May will notice that the colourings of the bricks and roof slates of this church, blend so well with the predominantly purple flowers of its surroundings. The churchyard has attracted also some memorial tree plantings over the years; unfortunately it lost its 117 year old cedar tree in the storm of January 1990. Tucked into a "corner" is the replica of a Holy Water fountain noticed near Igls in Austria, by Lady Selina Heathcote and Maria Trench whilst on holiday in 1845, [Maria later became the wife of Rev'd. R.F.Wilson]. A new incumbent in 1895 was Rev'd. Vere Awdry, whose hobby was model railway construction. His son Wilbert, [b.1910], who shared his interest, became the famous author of the 'Thomas The Tank Engine' books!

AMPORT
St. Mary

Here and there a flake of white falls from the painted scene,
Or a scowl of evergreen glares through the shroud... No movement else.

C. DAY. LEWIS 1904 - 1972

The snow muffles our feet as we trudge up the lane towards the church, but within the churchyard beneath the crystal carpet lies another carpet of whiteness waiting to reveal its annually repeated splendour, for already the snowdrops are awake... and will be a February flower festival for all to see.

It was in fact the high summer of 1957, when my wife Diana and I first came to Amport Church [she was a bridesmaid at a friend's wedding]. Little did we know then, that ten years later we would be living just a few miles away in Andover... and ever since.

Although St. Mary's was extensively restored in 1866, a substantial amount of the original, rendered, structure of the building remains [dated 1320-1330] and this can best be seen from the south-east corner of the churchyard. The delight of the window tracery, particularly the 'ogee' arch [the combination of a concave and convex form] together with the three 'mouchettes' forming a circle, are known as 'the Decorated style'. There is no better example of this period in the Test Valley, for it did not last long. The pinnacle of English power in Europe after the Battle of Crecy in 1346, was almost at once followed by the pestilence of 'The Black Death', which arrived in August 1348 and rapidly spread over the whole country.

Now therefore, open the gates of St. Mary's [A gift of the Royal Air Force] and stop for a moment to appreciate the form of this church, for it alone of all churches within Test Valley, apart from Romsey Abbey, retains its ancient Crossing Tower [above the crossing of the nave, chancel and transepts]. The honey coloured rendering brings warmth even to a winter picture.

Entering the church you cannot fail to notice Test Valley's most ornate font. A brass plaque informs that it was the gift of the Earl of Dudley in 1865 when on a visit to Amport House. The "intensely" carved wooden cover, we found raised, permitting a beautiful display of flowers to erupt from the font's depths. The west wall behind the font is entirely a Victorian extension and were it not for the clear glass of the window, the church would be quite a dark place, since all other windows are full of Victorian stained glass. The sanctuary has a 14th century three-seat sedilia on the south wall. The south transept, formerly the Marquis of Winchester's private pew, is now 'The children's chapel'. A memorial to the 15th Marquis [killed at the battle of Magersfontein in 1899] remains within, together with a framed copy of his funeral service, held here. The Band of the Coldstream Guards and the Choir of the Chapel Royal both took part in that service; it must have been quite impressive.

ANDOVER
St. Mary

There let the pealing organ blow
To the full-voiced quire below
In service high and anthems clear,
As may with sweetness, through mine ear,
Dissolve me into ecstasies,
And bring all Heaven before mine eyes.
il Penseroso. JOHN MILTON 1608 - 1674

Often referred to as the 'Cathedral of North Hampshire', St. Mary's is built in a commanding position above the town. The tower of the present church stands like a beacon, probably on the very site where in 994, Bishop Alphege of Winchester confirmed the Viking Chief, Olaf Triggvason... the man who subsequently began the Christian conversion of his homeland when he returned to Norway.

As previously mentioned, often our Test Valley churches are the personal gift of individual people... St. Mary's is one such church. It was in 1839 that Dr. Goddard [a former headmaster of Winchester College, who lived in Andover] wrote to the vicar that, 'he thought to do a kind act by the parish'. His anonymous offer was to pay for a completely new church if the Vestry Meeting found it acceptable. His offer was agreed to by them on 16th January 1840, and work began to demolish the original Norman church in November of that same year. The new church was sited slightly further to the east than the old one, so that services could continue there whilst the new one was constructed. Dr. Goddard had quite a lot of personal influence in its design; it is said that he very much admired Salisbury Cathedral, and probably therefore we can see the columns and the windows and the niches in the interior of the apse reflecting this, in what is a Victorian version of the Early English style. However, the design of the attractive semi-circular apse at the eastern end is not the same as Salisbury; it is more akin to examples which may be seen in 13th century continental cathedrals.

This church has a wonderful and colourful collection of mostly Victorian stained glass, in almost all of its groups of predominantly lancet windows. Of particular note are the three windows by the famous Mayer company of Munich. Latterly, in one pair of hitherto clear glass in the south-west corner, a Millennium window has been installed, designed and built by Mel Howse, entitled 'The Tree of Life'. A special folder, produced in 2002, is available for visitors containing information about every window in the building.

St. Mary's first architect, Mr. Augustus Livesay, suffered the embarrassment of having the south clerestory wall collapse during the construction and consequently a second consulting architect [Mr.S. Smirke, the designer of the British Museum], was appointed to oversee him and the remaining work. The opening service was held on 11th August 1844, but the tower was not completed until January 1846. Dr. Goddard died in October 1845 and is buried in the chancel of St. Mary's. A small portrait of the benefactor of this parish hangs in the Memorial Chapel, which occupies the entire north transept. In the south transept are hung the charity boards, with the details of earlier benefactions to the town, starting in 1569 with that of John Hanson Esq., whose name is perpetuated today in one of the town's secondary schools. Andover is by no means unique in this respect, for similar charity boards and the generosity of past benefactors that they record, can be seen in some other Test Valley churches, those at Chilworth and Hurstbourne Tarrant are good examples. Citizens of the town, who are appointed trustees of the charities, are still able to make grants to those inhabitants who suffer hardship or misfortune, or who have no one else to whom they can turn for a helping hand when in need. They are responsible also for the town's almshouses.

One of the chief delights of St. Mary's is its "music", whether given in the form of a short recital by a group of students from the neighbouring Cricklade College, or an evening concert by a visiting Symphony Orchestra. Sometimes the performers may be a visiting Welsh Choir, or a military band, and often a free lunchtime recital is given on *the pealing organ*, for it is a venue for all musical tastes throughout the whole year. It is truly a place worthy of John Milton's words, where each of us may think to ourselves, *dissolve me into ecstacies, and bring all Heaven before mine eyes*. Here it is achieved by the subtle blending of artistry and architecture.

ANDOVER
St. Michael and All Angels

In architecture as in all other operative arts, the end must direct the operation.
The end is to build well. Well building hath three conditions. Commodity, firmness and delight.

HENRY WOTTON 1568 - 1639

This is a spacious church for a "space age", built between 1962 and 1964. It lies almost surrounded by industrial buildings and new houses just off the Weyhill Road. The architect was Mr. R.A.P. Pinckney, a former pupil of Sir Giles Gilbert Scott the architect of Liverpool Cathedral. Mr. Pinckney built three other churches in Hampshire, all in the modern style; St. Barnabas, Weeke; All Hallows, Midanbury, and All Saints, Redbridge. All are very distinctive and different, but it is considered by many that St. Michael's, a well balanced cruciform plan, is the finest. Its wooden 40 foot copper-covered needle spire pierces the skyline, and makes a powerful "statement", especially when floodlit.

One must of course enter the church, to properly appreciate something which is quite unique within Test Valley... the vaulted ceiling. Painted a golden yellow, it is suspended in such a way as to create an interlocking pattern of arches over the entire roof space, at the centre of which [beneath the spire], it enfolds a pure white pointed cross in relief. The slender columns of artificial stone, which support the roof in the interior, are chamfered in such a way as to slowly change their shape from square at the base, to octagonal and back to square again at their summit. Hanging from the roof are clusters of lights described at the consecration service as being 'like a structure of atoms'... indeed, they do appear to change their relationship within their groups, as you move around the church beneath them.

The main door is at the north-west corner and one enters a 'narthex' or vestibule where, beneath the choir and organ gallery, the area is dominated by the beautiful white font of Portland stone. Likewise at the east end is another masterpiece in the same kind of stone... the altar. The delicate lines of its two supports making the whole seem more like a high-tech bridge, floating in mid-air against the back-drop of the dark, icy-green wall of Horton stone [about 180 million years old] from Edgehill in Oxfordshire. Above and behind this is the Lady Chapel and the new east window dedicated on 1st May 2004 entitled 'The Cross of Redeeming Love' [pictured on the back cover]. The lettering for the title; the In Memoriam plaque and the verses from Isaiah Chapter 40, were designed by Rod Hoyle of Romsey, and each letter was then beautifully hand-engraved by Patricia Hilton-Robinson of Amport.

The parish has come a long way from its beginnings as a Sunday School in somebody's house in 1875, which moved to a Mission Hut in 1885, and then into a dual-pupose brick Church Hall in 1936. Finally, thanks to the parishioners' vision and the architect's inspiration, a fine building has been achieved.

ANDOVER BAPTIST CHURCH

Here may the blind and hungry come, and light and food receive;
Here shall the lowliest guest have room, and see and taste and live.

ANNE STEELE 1717 - 1778

The Baptist Movement was founded by a group of 'separatists' from Gainsborough in Lincolnshire, led by John Smyth [a Cambridge graduate]. Persecuted during the reign of James I, they established themselves in Amsterdam in 1608. Other separatists from the same area later ventured to America as 'The Pilgrim Fathers'. Some of the first group, lead by Thomas Helwys, returned to London in 1612 and founded their first Baptist Church in Spitalfields, just outside the London Wall... their principle was religious toleration for all.

Later under the Protectorate of Oliver Cromwell, toleration for 'all who believe in Christ Jesus' did become the law. Two years after Charles II's return in 1660, an Act of Uniformity was passed, with the intention of further strengthening religious conformity, but all it succeeded in doing was consolidating religious Non-conformity as an enduring facet of Enlish life for centuries to come. A further Act of 1664, banned all meetings of more than five "dissenters". The Act of Indulgence [1672] tried to make amends, but not until the reign of William and Mary did times really change. The Act of Toleration [1689], permitting the building and licensing of meeting places for worship for Non-conformists, and the appointing of their own ministers, finally allowed the Baptists and other sects to grow.

It is thought that the Baptists in and around Andover joined with others in Whitchurch until 1824, when it is known that eleven members met together in premises in Andover High St., [but see under Andover U.R.C. for a slightly different version of events]. In 1828, they confidently organised an ecumenical Day of Prayer for the town with the other Non-conformists.

In 1866 it was decided to build a new Baptist church in the High Street and it was completed in May of the following year. It was quite large, having seating for over two hundred. The east end was decorated with two large arches one inside the other, on the highest arch was written ONE LORD.. ONE FAITH.. ONE BAPTISM, and on the inner one, ALL ONE IN CHRIST JESUS.

The church florished under minister Joseph Haslar from 1871-1895. He kept the position of Secretary of the Southern Baptist Union until the age of 93 in 1922!

Andover's Town Development Scheme in the 1960's affected access to the church, and a developer offered to build the present church, in exchange for the High Street site. The new church is remarkable in providing within, an excellent uninterrupted space. This is a church which, in the words of their Mission Statement, is 'Seeking to be a dynamic Christ-like community'. I'm sure the founder members would have approved.

ANDOVER METHODIST CHURCH

Forth in Thy name, O Lord I go,
My daily labour to pursue;
Thee, only Thee, resolved to know,
In all I think, or speak, or do.

CHARLES WESLEY 1707 - 1788

In the summer of 1751 two horses with their riders might have been seen taking the route from Reading to Salisbury via Andover; a man and a woman on one horse, [Rev'd and Mrs. John Wesley] and a Mr. Blackwell on the other... Methodism had arrived in Hampshire. Mr. Blackwell stopped to preach in Andover and John Wesley and his wife journeyed on to Salisbury. Of course it is well known that John Wesley was an Anglican priest; he had been ordained in 1728 and had gone to Oxford to complete his college fellowship. Here he joined his brother Charles and two other students and together they formed a religious study group, they became known as Methodists, because of their obvious devotion and "methodical" approach to learning. Whilst at Oxford they expanded their Christian work, to bring comfort and help particularly to poor people and those in workhouses and prisons.

The Wesley brothers both left Oxford in 1735 and John was invited to work for the Society for the Propagation of the Gospel [S.P.G.] in America among the ethnic Indians; he was not a success and returned to London at the end of 1737. A few months later he went in his own words 'unwillingly to a society in Aldersgate St. and heard one reading Luther's preface to the Epistle to the Romans... I felt my heart strangely warmed'. He never looked back from that moment; he had found his vocation and needed little urging from that other great pillar of Methodism, George Whitfield, 'to go to the unchurched masses'. Wesley's aim was to keep the Methodist Movement part of the Anglican Church, but there were always tensions, for example regarding the licensing of lay preachers, and after his death in 1791, the Society soon became totally independent. Unfortunately this gave rise to further fragmentation when the Primitive Methodists separated from the Wesleyans in 1811; not until 1932 was the breach healed and Methodist unity regained.

The establishment of a Methodist congregation in Andover took some time to evolve; it is thought that their first meeting place was in a store on the corner of Shepherd's Spring Lane. However by 1818 the first Andover Wesleyan 'circuit' was formed, with thirteen different societies and a total membership of 204. In 1819 a vacant site was purchased in Winchester Street, on which the first Wesleyan Church was built, with the adjoining property No. 16, as the minister's home. George Wallis and W.Wiltshire formed a Primitive Methodist Society and in 1836 built their chapel in East Street. Their circuit was formed in 1837 with 340 members and four travelling preachers... one of the widest circuits in the Primitive Methodist Connexion. When the present church in Bridge Street was completed in 1906, the Winchester Street Church became the Salvation Army Citadel. The design of the Bridge Street Church surely reflects the Anglican background of Methodism, in its strongly traditional Perpendicular style and its flint and stone external appearance. Inside, the refurbishment of 1996 has re-created the familiar warm and welcoming environment with a greater flexibility of space.

The prominent site right next to the River Anton was obtained from one of the many stalwarts of Wesleyan Methodism, who established their own businesses in the town, namely Benjamin Baverstock Pond. In 1902 he had become the first Methodist Mayor of the town and he was also a County Councillor. He was not alone in his interest in civic affairs, Cllr. Will McLoughlin another Methodist, was Mayor in the following year. They were among many who epitomised the Protestant work ethic, and for whom their faith was very much part of their business lives, as they put Christianity into practice, perhaps in the words of the hymn above... and prospered thereby. Others are copying their example today.

In 1957 another Methodist church was built in the Weyhill Road in recognition of the expansion of the town to the west, and named St. Andrew's because it was opened on St. Andrew's Day. A further extension to this church was opened by George Thomas [the former speaker of the House of Commons, later Lord Tonypandy], on 30th November 1985. Methodism has come a long way since Wesley passed through on his horse!

ANDOVER ROMAN CATHOLIC CHURCH
St. John the Baptist

The next day John the Baptist seeth Jesus coming unto him and saith,
Behold the Lamb of God, which taketh away the sins of the world.

The Gospel according to ST. JOHN Chap 1 Verse 29

In a pleasant residential area of the town, St. John the Baptist Catholic Church is an excellent example of the mid-20th Century style of architecture, being similar to that of St. Michael's Anglican Church half a mile away. It was built just five years earlier [1957]. The foundation stone was laid by Archbishop J. H. King on 22nd May, and beneath the stone was placed a copper cylinder with details of the event and a set of coins of the realm. The first service to be held in the new church was on Christmas Eve 1958.

The church is positioned on a north/south axis, and has an unusual bow shaped roof line, which is apparent in the closely boarded ceiling inside and in the shape of the large north and south windows. The entrance is at the southern end and consists of a vestibule, within which, we particularly noticed a map of the parish, showing that it extends from Shipton Bellinger to Whitchurch in one direction, and from Stockbridge to Linkenholt in the other!

The nave is entered centrally from the vestibule, through another set of glass doors and beneath an upper gallery; the fine Portland Stone font on the left in the picture, is now [2005] placed centrally near the entrance. The impresssive north wall of the sanctuary, which is entirely of glass, contains in its inner five panels the stained glass representation of 'The Risen Christ' by Paul Jefferies, which we are informed was financed either wholly or in part by donations from American sevicemen stationed in the area during World War II. This 'vivid and powerfully compelling' window has Christ robed in blue; the predominantly red background is streaked with gold from the sun. Seven white doves of peace fly out from the tree of life. Its impact is made more noticeable, by the lack of any windows in the nave apart from small clerestory windows along the length of the side walls. The eastern transept, like the north aspect, is similarly glazed from floor to ceiling, but not in coloured glass.

On the opposite side is a memorial wall-plaque to the 'BLESSED JOHN BODEY MARTYR OF ANDOVER 2nd, November 1583'. He was born in Wells in Somerset, and having been educated in Winchester and Oxford, he went to the English College at Douai in France where he studied law. After returning to England in 1580, he was arrested and hanged in Andover for 'denying the supremacy of Queen Elizabeth in spiritual matters'. His was a fate sometimes also shared by those of a Puritan persuasion during Elizabeth's reign. Also, no doubt, his punishment was probably influenced by the hostility of King Philip of Spain towards England, and the threat of the Armada.

ANDOVER
UNITED REFORMED CHURCH

Were the whole realm of nature mine, that were an offering far too small;
Love so amazing, so Divine, demands my soul, my life, my all.

ISAAC WATTS 1674 - 1748

The United Reformed Church was established on 5th October 1972, to unite the Congregationalists and the Presbyterians. Both Churches had been born in the days of the Reformation, but differed in their concepts of church governance, and both grew from the consequences of the Act of Uniformity of 1662. This required all ministers of religion to be re-ordained if not previously ordained by a bishop, and that all should accept the use of the Book of Common Prayer. Those ministers who had not been properly ordained, and would not comply with the Act, were dispossessed of their "living", or parish.

The years 1662 to 1689 were the "wilderness" years for both groups, they had to meet furtively mostly at night, illegally, in barns, cellars or in woods, as the Andover group did in a dell in Harewood Forest. Later they met in a cottage in Sopers Lane, which they shared on alternate Sundays with the Presbyterians.

Since preaching was banned, the Congregationalist Isaac Watts, came up with the idea of "singing the faith", and so good was his poetry that his hymns are still sung today. Employment in the 'professions' was also banned to Non-conformists, so they turned their energies to trade and business; notably, some national chocolate manufacturers came into being, [Fry, Cadbury, and Rowntree], and the Lloyd and Barclay families turned to banking, whereas the Clark family made shoes.

After the accession of William and Mary in 1688 things improved, and thanks to the generosity of Mr. Bunny, the Andover Congregationalists were given a site just off East Street where 'The Upper Meeting House' was built in 1700. In 1824 it is recorded that 'some members of the Baptist persuasion left, and built their own place of worship in the High St. which opened in December of that year'. An attempt to expand into Abbotts Ann at the invitation of the local blacksmith, Robert Tasker, met with considerable opposition from the Anglican community, and serious rioting took place. However, local opposition became the spur to industrial success, for Tasker was forced to go further afield to find work. In a very short time he was nationally known for the innovation and quality of his products.

In 1830 they purchased the ministers house next door to the church, and then in 1839, a considerable enlargement of the church took place. A pipe organ was purchased, which is believed to have come from the St. George's Chapel in the private appartments at Windsor Castle. Happily both the house and the church still stand. The original galleries are still in use, supported on Tasker columns in this, the oldest church building in Andover.

APPLESHAW
St. Peter

And make us as Newton was,
who in his garden watching
the apple falling towards England, became aware
between himself and her, of an eternal tie.

W.H. AUDEN 1907 - 1973

The name Appleshaw, conjures up for me a scene redolent of blossom and bees and warm breezes, where springtime is eternal. For such a romantic fantasy I hope I may be excused, but the truth is, that this little village tucked into the folds of a gentle countryside to the north and west of Andover was, it seems, probably renown for its fruit trees from the earliest times. The Norman name "Appelleshaghe" reflected an even older one "Appel shaugh", where shaugh meant wood. The Romans introduced apples into 'Britannia', and there are sufficient remains of Roman villas in the area around here, for their cultivation by the settlers to have been more than a possibility. The discovery of the 'Appleshaw Hoard' of Roman pewter tableware marked with Christian symbols, now in the British Museum, shows that there existed here, one of the very first Christian communities [in about the year 350].

The present St. Peter's Church was built in 1830. The former church, probably dating from around 1200 was always subordinate to Amport, as was the new one until Appleshaw became a parish in its own right in 1866. A plaque inside the church, recalls the gift of money given by the same Society that assisted with West Tytherley's rebuilding, explaining that because of this, 86 of the 271 places in the church would be forever 'free'. On the plaque are the names of the churchwarden of that time, George Redman, and the architect Mr. Sturmer. I subsequently noticed Mr. Redman's rather grand tomb surrounded by iron railings, to the left of the pathway as one approaches the front door.

I also recognised that the windows of St. Peter's are similar in design to those in St. Denys, Chilworth, and the Baptist Church in Romsey; one wonders if the same Mr. Sturmer was responsible? Thoughtfully placed inside the porchway for visitors like myself, was an old photograph, which shows that originally there was another small belfry tower on the top of the existing tower, and on top of that, a short spire... there is also a drawing of the old church. On display here also, inviting examination, is presumed to

be the old font. Even though it is only nine inches across, yet it has its own stone-carved cover, resting beside it. Just inside the door into the church itself, is another font which certainly came from St. Mary's Andover, probably designed for that church by Mr. Livesay between 1840 and 1844. It is octagonal in shape with free-standing decorative columns, and presumably must have been donated by St. Mary's at the time of the re-ordering of the Andover church in the early 1870's.

Once inside St. Peter's, there is a cool, somewhat austere freshness, which is complemented by the pastel shades of opaque glass predominant in the diamond-paned windows, except that is for the window that faces you at the east end of the chancel. This is in memory of Mary Stock, who died in 1949, and is a glorious expression of Christ in Majesty, rich in colour and was installed in 1952. The nave and chancel are about the same size and length, and the two transepts built at their junction not much smaller, though that on the south side is partitioned off to form a vestry. Some 18th century memorials from the previous church remain fixed to the chancel walls, one in particular recalls the death of the only son of the Butcher family who was just eleven years old, when he was 'drowned trying to save the life of a schoolfellow'. On the wall opposite, which I assume to be actually part of the original church, there is partly revealed behind the plaster finish, the first two phrases of The Lord's Prayer painted on the wall; one has to wonder if the rest is still there and if it too could be similarly exposed to view?

If you visit at the right time of the year, do not depart before walking around the church to see the wonderful carpet of snowdrops and winter aconites at the eastern end of the churchyard, and then after passing out of the gate overhung by its protective yew tree, perhaps turn again before crossing over the little stream, to see it as the photograph shows it shortly after its exterior repainting in 1997, the only 'primrose yellow' church in Test Valley...repainted again in 2010 in cream and grey.

ASHLEY
St. Mary

A thing of beauty is a joy for ever: Its loveliness increases; it will never
pass into nothingness; but still will keep a quiet bower for us,...

JOHN KEATS 1795 - 1821

Little more than a mile due east of Kings Somborne, this little gem of a church lies on one of those precious lanes that link England with its soul. The church is set above the level of the road and if you come at the right time of year, the bank up which the little pathway climbs to the entrance door, is a sea of cowslips.

May you enter here with the words above, or some other suitable lines learned "by heart" in a half-forgotten school-room, and you will be rewarded I'm sure... it seems a poetic place. The Pilgrim Crosses on the door arch are evidence of former visitors in whose steps you are treading. Once you open the heavy creaking door and step down into the nave, revealed before you is a coolness and calmness often unobtainable in this modern world. We appreciated the welcoming posy of fresh flowers on the square Norman font.

Although services in this church are only promulgated for Easter, Harvest and Christmas Day, the evidence of care is everywhere; the freshly-swept floor tiles, a window set ajar to freshen the air and the eight polished pews comfortably seating perhaps only sixteen persons in total. From here, in the narrowest of naves in the whole of Test Valley [hardly twelve feet wide], one may then pass through the narrowest of chancel arches, which though reputedly Norman, reminds us of some of those beautiful

Saxon arches in even older Hampshire churches. The gently upward-sloping floor of the chancel is a significant feature, and glancing around you will see in the splay of the window on the south side, a medieval wall painting of St. Mary, to whom of course the church is dedicated. On the walls are two marble plaques of the 18th century... one for the chief surgeon to three kings, Charles II, James II and William III.

Through the 15th century east window and the tiny lancet windows on either side, the light floods in from the beautiful open Hampshire sky; there is no stained glass, but the remains of two old windows high up in the south nave wall, rediscovered during repair work and looking more like portholes, <u>do</u> have engraved glass.

At the west end of the nave were two display cases with items of historic interest and another containing a model of the site, which showed how things might have looked as part of a castle complex... outside only the vaguest earthen ramparts remain. There is an oak post incorporating an alms-box said to be of mid 17th century origin, but possibly older, which used to stand like a sentinel on the end of the last pew. Today, one's offering may be placed in a more secure place in the wall next to the holy water stoop. This church remains in the care of the Churches Conservation Trust.

AWBRIDGE
All Saints

In the rush and noise of life, as you have intervals, step within yourselves and be still. Wait upon God and feel His good presence:

WILLIAM PENN 1644 - 1718.

Awbridge Parish was formed in 1877 out of the original Parish of Michelmersh. All Saints Church, [architect, Mr. Colson] being conceived by Rev'd. Thomas Heathcote Tragett, its first incumbent and principal sponsor. It is constructed of brick and faced with Swanage stone in a typical Victorian Gothic Decorated style. It lies in Church Lane [where else could it be?], off the undulating, and quite busy Danes Road.

A smart gravel path leads to the north door, through a churchyard partly conserved as a wild-flower meadow. Inside, there is a feeling of quiet spaciousness, not a sound intrudes. At the western end is an open carpeted area, of which the main feature is the font, bathed in light from nearly all sides, but chiefly from the group of clear glass windows in the west wall through which, the whole panoply of the leaves of the surrounding beech trees can be fully appreciated. On this west wall a plaque records the way in which this parish marked the Millenium... donations were given to the Christian Blind Mission, 'sufficient to pay to restore sight to 2000 people in East Africa'.

The windows in both sides of the nave are memorials of one sort or another, all are in stained glass of the 20th century, ranging in date from 1922 to 1965. The subjects are traditional, except for the one of the boy Jesus in his father's carpentry shop. The more impressive east window of 1887 is a "rood" scene, [Christ on the cross, with Mary and St. John standing on either side], which was given in commemoration of the Rev'd.Tragett. I particularly liked the south side sanctuary window in memory of Anne Tragett, showing the Virgin Mary with a passage from the Magnificat.

The chancel arch is high and pointed and springs on either side from two stone corbels of pierced clusters of leaves; the moulding on the outside of the arch, is completed by two stone carved heads in a medieval style. The interior of the chancel is wood-panelled up to a height of about eight feet, with two pews incorporated at the sides, thus creating a wide carpeted area for worship activity, children's plays, or recitals. There is a fine wooden pulpit, and it is enhanced by a three branched brass candelabra and a brass book-rest.

The photograph shows a south-west extension, generously provided in the late 1980's by a non-Anglican local family, who worshipped here. I mention this only because it emphasises the churchwarden's words to me... "We hold ecumenical services here, everyone in the village of whatever denomination is welcome." Indeed I could tell, the church is a well-used social, cultural and religious venue.

BARTON STACEY
All Saints

Walk there awhile, before the day is done
Beneath the banner and the battered casque,
Where graven heraldry is bronze and stone
With lily and with cross and leopard's mask
Spandrils the arch. Thou shalt not walk alone.

MURIEL STUART 1885 - 1967

We would certainly encourage you to *walk there awhile before day is done...* so park the car and enter the village shop, for this is where to obtain the "necessaries of life", and importantly, the necessary key to the church. All Saints stands proudly at the crossroads in the very centre of the village, as we see it today it has the external apprearance given to it by the Victorian reconstruction of 1877, but behind the surface the original walls of 1250 still exist, and in some places the original windows; the oldest in the north wall of the north transept. The 15th century one just to the east of the porch, apparently has a Latin inscription in the outer sill which translated means 'Here [below] lies the body of John P...' thereby doubling as a memorial, but to be honest we could not easily read it ourselves.

The early history of All Saints is fragmentary; a research document available on a convenient table inside, records that perhaps a Saxon or Norman church on this site was dedicated to St. Victor. The most impressive external feature is the tower, within which is a fine west window probably of a date around 1540. This tower together with its contemporary in Longparish and a later one at Kimpton, are the only three in the whole of Test Valley with external stair turrets, which are separately visible above the outline of the top of the tower. This tower is built entirely of dressed stone and has pinnacles as well as being battlemented, whereas Longparish and Kimpton lack these further embellishments.

Once inside, we found there was very definitely a "military feel" to this church. For a start, at the western end of the nave where the structure of the tower intrudes into the church, there are two huge hatchments placed either side of the tower archway... an heraldic dream for any connoisseur of such items. Below them tastefully grouped are another dozen or so smaller modern badges on shields, presented by army units, which at one time or another were based at the military camp or other places nearby. If you glance back at the entrance you will see above the door another large board, on which the Royal Arms of George III are displayed. Just inside the door on the left as you enter, is the square topped Norman font with a lovely carved wooden cover, said to have been made up in 1870 from part of the chancel screen of neighbouring Longparish Church, and on which is recorded that it was 'restored in 1974 by students of the construction wing of the Royal School of Military Engineering'. Another small brass plate on the wall of the north aisle tells you that 'extensive restoration work was carried out on this church by soldiers of the 12th Engineer Brigade... in 1971'. They all deserve our grateful thanks.

A more poignant reminder of the price of military service is provided by the memorial [also on the same wall] of two sons of the Hodgson family of "Gravelacre", who died within six days of eachother in 1915. As you continue your stroll, if you glance at the bible on the lectern, you will see it is presented in memory of Acting-sublieutenant Leopold Johnstone who went down with his ship H.M.S. Invincible at the Battle of Jutland on 31st May 1916. There are some real, and rare, medieval floor tiles in the sanctuary and many of them are similar in pattern to those in the retrochoir of Winchester Cathedral.

Unusually, the two aisles of this church have been allowed to extend and almost completely "absorb" the north and south transepts, and since therefore the chancel is now between the transepts, the clear unimpeded light from their windows, floods into the choir in a very special and unique way. The contrast with neighbouring Longparish is remarkable, but each church retains an individuality and a presence that only a visit will satisfy.

We enjoyed our visit and even remembered to return the key!

BOSSINGTON
St. James

Now lords, for France! The enterprise whereof shall be to you, as us, like glorious...
let us deliver our puissance into the hand of God, putting it straight in expedition.
King Henry V . WILLIAM SHAKESPEARE 1564 - 1616

If we return in our imagination to those days of 1415, when it is known that Henry V's army was encamped in the fields around this church prior to leaving for France, we might have seen the monarch himself attending Mass in the original church on this very spot. Sadly nothing remains of that church, the present one having been built in 1839 by the owner of Bossington House, John Meggett Elwes. Sadly also, nothing remains of the village that once surrounded it, though this was not the result of The Black Death plague as can often be the case, but of the whim of the previous owner of the estate in 1823. He was an M.P. for Southampton, Mr. Penlease, for whom the sight of the humble cottages of his workers 'spoiled his view'. He dismissed them, and in a short time they had all been forced to find work <u>and</u> accommodation elsewhere... and down came the cottages. The church he could <u>not</u> destroy, but having no parishioners it soon fell into ruin, until the estate was bought by the generous new owner in 1835, and he decided to restore it. He imported the Swanage stone for both walls and roof, as had been used in the original building.

The photograph, which was taken when the frost was glistening 'on wood and iron and stone', shows that the church stands on a three-foot platform which raises it above the flood-plain of the River Test. It lies at the end of a little avenue of lime trees, which may once have been the village street, leading from the Houghton to Mottisfont road.

It is a compliment to Mr. Elwes' vision that today "his" church is still in use. Inside, in deference to its history, the Royal Arms of Henry V carved in wood, are fixed to the west wall. The Tudor Rose carvings of the pew ends commemorate yet another royal visit to this place... by Queen Elizabeth I, during her stay at Pittleworth Manor nearby. One might think its place in history was thereby assured by these two royal visits, but there is more. During the building of the Andover to Redbridge Canal, a ceremonial ring worn by a former bishop in Saxon times [thought to be of the 9th century] was found here, and before this in 1783, a relic of even earlier times was discovered... a 'pig of lead', stamped with the mark of the Roman Emperor Nero. Presumably it fell from a cart here, during its transportation from the Mendip Hills to Southampton and thence to Rome. Once this was clearly a place on the 'highway of history'.

We are as much a part of this landscape as the invisible villagers of the past; we should ensure that we protect it for those who come after us.

BRAISHFIELD
All Saints

The works of the Lord are great, sought out of all of them that have pleasure therein.
His work is honourable and glorious and His righteousness endureth for ever.

PSALM 111 verses 2 - 3

I saw the first verse of the words above, on a gravestone in this churchyard... that of Archibald Henry Swinton. He was an entomologist and naturalist, who from 1913-1916 contributed weekly articles to local papers, on subjects varying from the effect of sun-spots on floods and famine, to butterflies and potatoes.

All Saints Church was built by the famous Victorian architect William Butterfield in 1855, during the period when he was engaged on building what has been called 'England's most celebrated and most expensive Victorian Church, All Saints, Margaret Street', [near Oxford Street in London]. Butterfield used a contrasting diamond pattern on the upper part of the external walls here, as he did also on the Royal Hampshire County Hospital. From outside the church, the only indication of a chancel inside, is the single buttress and the more ornate treatment of the window to its right, compared with the windows of the nave. On the north side of the church the roof line continues to a lower level over a small north aisle, in memory of Mrs. Caroline Davies, wife of the Rev'd. James Davies 'chief promoter of this church'... as explained on the east window, which is his own memorial. There is an interesting tile pattern to the roof, and at its apex, possessing a very smart clock, is the shingled bell turret, dated 1902.

Inside the porch is the painted text, 'Enter His gates with thanksgiving, and into His courts with praise'... I did so, and at once admired the lovely beamed and boarded ceiling of dark wood in what seemed to be pristine condition; I'm sure the donor of the original restoration in 1945 would have been pleased to see it. The highly decorated and gilded east wall also makes an immediate impact; this shows Christ in Majesty above the central of the three lancet windows, with the four gospel evangelists beneath, two on either side. This is the largest and most impressive mural in Test Valley, and was the gift of Mr. J.E. Pepper of Jermyns in 1906.

The chancel, almost invisible from the outside, is understated inside also, one has to look closely to see that the roof supporting beams <u>do</u> descend to corbels at this point. At floor level it is more obvious, for the choir stalls and all wooden fittings here, can only be described as most elaborate. They were made by Thomas and Co. of Winchester, and hand-carved in the church itself by a lady, who was a guest of the donor, Mrs. Dodgson of Braishfield House, whilst doing her work. The faculty for this work was granted in June 1909. The panelled walls of the sanctuary came from Romsey Abbey; an invoice among the parish records held in the County Record Office, confirms this, dated 29th January 1914.

BROUGHTON
St. Mary

Give me a calm and thankful heart,
From every murmur free;
The blessings of Thy grace impart,
And let me live in Thee.

ANNE STEELE 1717 - 1778

One of the best ways to discover Broughton is probably on foot, starting in a northerly direction from some point on the old Roman road that runs across the Broughton Ridge to the south of the village. By so doing, whether on the Clarendon Way Footpath or some other convenient route, you will come across one of the finest views in all Hampshire as you come to the breast of the escarpment. At once you find the valley of the Wallop Brook and the village itself laid out below you, with Danebury Hill in the middle distance. If by chance it is one of those days when the wind is in the north-west, the clarity of the air, sharp and clear as crystal, will enable you almost "to reach out and touch" the North Wessex Downs ahead of you... and away to the right, you may see also the hills around Petersfield, even though they are up to 25 miles away.

Right in the centre of the village the sturdy tower of St. Mary's Church forms a focus for this community as it has done for centuries. The features of the present church mostly derive from considerable extensions that were added to the original building between 1190 and 1220. The western entrance and door of that time [now blocked] was later incorporated into the corner-buttressed tower when that was added in the 15th century. Entry today is gained by one or other of the two porches on the north and south side of the nave. I used the latter, within which I found a triptych style War Memorial, which Parr and Sewter's fine book about the village, records as being made of wood and copper from H.M.S. Britannia. On its pediment were the words 'For King and Country' in gold lettering, and on either side was a Roll of Honour with its title lettering painted in red, to list 'The Heroic Dead'.

Inside the church the balance and charm of the building are immediately apparent, art and architecture combining to produce a special warmth and welcome. I recommend that you first admire the solid marble font almost in your path [date 1879] in memory of Dr. Fox, and there is also a window to his memory subscribed by 600 of his friends; on the wall close by are a number of framed lists of baptisms since 1932. I was sad not to see the beautiful triptych that I saw on the altar in the south aisle on a previous visit, but the modern three panelled Broughton Dovecot 'wallhanging' on the wall of the north aisle facing me, was just the same as ever, fresh and as evocative as on the day it was made as can be seen opposite. The sun filtered through the clerestory windows and highlighted in the adjoining pews, the two eight-foot high wrought-iron and brass candelabra of 1904, that once must have stood in the sanctuary. 1904 was a year of much adornment for St. Mary's... the very fine east window depicting the adoration of the shepherds is of this date, as are the other chancel windows, though of lesser quality. I suspect the two riddel posts surmounted by golden angels in the sanctuary are of this date too; a photograph in the helpful guide folder, shows that once there were four. Under the south sanctuary window stands a most remarkable pillar piscina, quite the finest and probably the oldest in Test Valley; it is adorned with roses and 'grotesque figures'!

In the churchyard on the south side is the tomb of Anne Steele, a lifetime resident of this village and celebrated hymn-writer, one of whose verses is written above. Her father William, was co-pastor of Broughton Baptist Chapel in 1699. Further details of the long-standing witness of the Baptists of Broughton can be found on the page following upon this one.

By pausing for a moment outside the church and looking over to Broughton House where Anne spent her last years, we can easily imagine the agreeable scene that gave rise to her many compositions.

If you can, I would advise you to come back one day and hear the bells, two of the six dating from the time of James I, echoing across the valley, calling the faithful to worship. Up to 1963 the curfew bell was tolled daily during the winter months, sounding in Thomas Gray's famous words 'the knell of parting day' from this very tower, warning the owners of thatched cottages to attend to their fires before retiring.

BROUGHTON BAPTIST CHURCH

Father of mercies in Thy word what endless glory shines,
For ever be Thy name adored for these celestial lines.

ANNE STEELE 1717 - 1778

The phrase, *In Thy word what endless glory shines*, from the above verse, are carved most appropriately, above and beneath an open book [signifying a Bible], on the front face of the oak lectern of this church. It was presented on the 250th anniversary of the birth of their author Anne Steele, the daughter of one of the first pastors of this church; a well-known hymn writer who lived here in Broughton.

The history of the church starts with the meetings in various village cottages, now confidently thought to date from about 1651. The first documentary proof exists in a minute book recording the gathering of some eighty-five persons as 'The Porton and Broughton Church', in the village of Porton in Wiltshire in 1653. By 1687 the church had grown considerably and members are recorded as coming from Amesbury, Winchester, Abbotts Ann and Bulford.

In 1704, the Broughton and Wallop "friends" amicably decided to separate from the others, and began to meet every Sunday in Broughton under the leadership of Henry Steele, who remained the pastor here until his death in 1739. Henry Steele and his nephew William [the father of Anne] were timber merchants, who supplied timber to the Royal Naval Dockyard in Portsmouth. On the site of the present church were two cottages, donated by Henry and adapted by his brother Thomas as a meeting house, together with land for a burial ground behind them.

In 1809 Pastor Russell arrived from Bristol College and by 1816 the membership had outgrown the cottages and a new church was constructed on the site. A legacy received in 1817 enabled the gallery to be added inside the new building. Like Henry Steele before him, Hugh Russell was pastor here for forty years and among other things he started the village school in the rooms at the back of the church in 1835.

An old photograph of the church taken in 1898 shows a rather plain brick building... the present classical appearance dates from 1926 and certainly gives a certain grandeur to the church. Inside, old pews reputedly made from timbers salvaged from the wreck of 'The Royal George' in 1782, remain. Two carpeted aisles divide the pews and lead forward to a slightly raised dais. We noticed a lovely old communion table standing at the side and above it, a more recent gift from the village's "twin-town" of Sauve in the south of France; a wooden Huguenot Cross.

Sadly since the time of our visit, we have to report that this church has been closed... perhaps the spirit of Anne Steele will one day see to its re-opening.

BULLINGTON
St. Michael and All Angels

Reserved, shy, but full of significance, it hid whatever it might hold behind a
veil, keeping it till the hour should come, and with the hour, those who were called and chosen.

The Wind in The Willows. KENNETH GRAHAME 1859 - 1932

The approach to Bullington Church along the valley of the River Dever, brings one into an intimacy with that quiet little stream that never fails to remind me of the words above. Although dawn had passed by the time I arrived, Grahame's lines about the animals' destination could so very easily apply here... *Reserved, shy, but full of significance, it hid whatever it might hold behind a veil, keeping it till the hour should come...*

It was indeed fairly early on a clear late autumn morning when I had my first glimpse of St. Michael's, but the veil of early morning mist had disappeared. I opened the gates [the gift of an American family] and took the path down through the little avenue of limes to the church door. As with very many early churches its origins are lost in time, but a walk around the outside, will reveal possibly two little Saxon windows at the west end of the nave one on each side, and on the north side a very definite Norman doorway, now blocked up.

The basic structure of the church is of the 12th and 13th centuries, but it is clear that a lot of restoration work was done in the 19th century. From the Victorian porch on the south side, one steps down into the nave; opposite, the blocked north door has been formed into a niche and within it hangs a framed history. To the left, the area underneath the tower is both the Baptistry and where the

two bells are rung, it is lit by stained glass west windows, appropriately depicting the baptism of Christ, and Christ with the children. In the quatrefoil above is a dove representing the descent of the Holy Spirit. At the opposite end of the nave, the stained glass east window records the restoration work of 1871 and is very similar in style, design and colour to those in St. Mark's, Ampfield by William Wailes.

The nave is centrally lit by four wooden hanging candelabra each with six holders, having a cross at their centre and suspended from a small metal crown. The pews are of pine but the choir stalls are of oak and integral with them is a three branch oak and brass candelabra at the Vicar's stall. The altar is of oak also and upon it stands a pair of quite beautiful brass candlesticks and a cross from Stratfield Saye.

The church was originally built by the Lord of the Manor for his family and estate workers as a private chapel. The first records apparently tell that the Manor of Bolendum [Bullington] was given in 1008 by King Ethelred to the abbey at Wherwell, which is just a little way down-stream, and that this connection remained intact until the Dissolution of that "Monastery" in 1540. The abbey was destroyed, but this little church survived... long may it continue to do so.

CHARLTON
St. Thomas

Guard well within yourself that treasure... kindness;
Know how to give without hesitation,
How to lose without regret;
How to acquire without meanness.

GEORGE SAND 1804 - 1876

From our perspective in the 21st century these words seem to be especially appropriate for the Rev'd. Dr. William Stanley Goddard D.D., a former headmaster of Winchester College, who retired to Andover in 1809. Before ever he came to be involved with the reconstruction of the Parish Church of St. Mary's, and the building of the National Schools in East Street, he was the benefactor of the out-lying chapel of that parish at Foxcotte. It is reported that in the early part of the 19th century the building was in a ruinous condition, and so it was through his initiative that restoration work was completed in 1812. Nearly one hundred years later in 1907, it was thought that since the population of Foxcotte was now only thirty-three, it would be better if the church could be relocated in the centre of the new village at Charlton, less than a mile away. After careful deliberation the decision was made, and the process of transferring most of the materials from the old church to the new began, cart-load by cart-load. Attempts to pull down the tower failed and it remains to this day on the original site, now part of a private dwelling.

It did not take long for the new church to be built, the foundation stone was laid on 3rd March 1908 and the consecration service was held on 19th of August of the same year. The wisdom of moving the church, doubted by some at the time, was probably seen to have been vindicated by the growth of Charlton during the last century, but the growth has now almost reached out to engulf the old church site, so perhaps with hindsight it could have stayed where it was! Like the tide, populations also ebb and flow... we live on a moving planet and need to remember that too, from time to time. We get used to the idea of our rotating Earth giving us night and day, and year by year moving around our Sun, but do we stop to consider that our Sun is itself an infinitesimally small part of a vaster, ever moving galaxy and is inexorably "towing" us through space quite literally 'into the

unknown' every moment of our lives! Are not those now famous words of Minnie Louise Haskins, quoted by King George VI in his Christmas broadcast in 1939, still relevant to us today? '...And I said to the man who stood at the gate of the year: "Give me a light that I may tread safely into the unknown," And he replied: "Go out into the darkness and put your hand into the hand of God. That shall be to you, better than a light and safer than a known way"... Does not that response touch a chord in each and every one of us, who seek to find a reason for his or her own place in "the scheme of things"? The darkness is the darkness of space, and though we may differ in what we assume God to be, we do not need to wonder why as human beings on our involuntary journey, we find the need to set aside "Holy Places", where we may try to come to terms with the imponderable majesty and power of our universe. If we ignore our innermost feelings and our churches, it is in 1939 terms, like putting up the blackout curtains and pretending we are safe!

St. Thomas' is a delightful building, we particularly liked the Baptistry apse at the west end, domed in stone, and the little stone figure of St. Thomas, high above in a special niche on the nave wall at this end. The floor is of parquet wood blocks with a central blue-carpeted aisle, and the same carpet is laid wall-to-wall in the sanctuary, which has to be curtained off during the week when the nave is in use as a community hall. Integral in the north side of the chancel arch is the foundation stone with three consecration crosses... a small display box holds the tiny silver trowel and mallet that was used by Miss Mary Jane Poore to lay it. The stained glass east window of St. Michael in medieval armour, is a memorial to the architect, Hugh Benson, who was killed in Flanders in 1915 aged thirty-one. Apart from the 1998 extension on the north side [replacing an earlier one built in 1978], it remains as he designed it... an even greater memorial.

CHILBOLTON
St. Mary the Less

Now fades the glimmering landscape on the sight,
And all the air a solemn stillness holds...

Elergy Written in a Country Churchyard.
THOMAS GREY 1716 - 1771

This is the only church dedicated to 'St. Mary The Less' in Test Valley. There are ten to St. Mary, or St. Mary The Virgin, referring of course to the mother of Jesus... my belief is that St. Mary the Less refers to Mary of Magdala or Mary Madalene, who according to St. Mark's Gospel was the first person to whom Jesus appeared, after his ressurection on the first Easter morning. I have read that she is the patron saint of 'repentant sinners' and 'the contemplative life'.

The church is situated at one end of a most charming village, just where you might expect to find it, welcoming you if you arrive from the east and bidding you farewell and "God's blessing" if you are departing. A small green separates it from a cluster of thatched cottages on one side, and the water meadows of the River Test lie beyond it on the opposite side.

My favourite approach is a delightful walk from the direction of Chilbolton Common. Close to where the first main stream of the Test is bridged, you can take a path alongside the water and over a stile, then across the water meadows using the church steeple as a beacon to guide you... you can't go wrong. It is perfect on a summer evening with the warm setting sun on your back, and the insects dancing over the reeds at the water's edge, seemingly oblivious of the swallows who race to and fro' to catch a meal for their young. If you are too late for the walk, you may see the church as in the top photograph, for after sunset when the flood-lighting comes on, it then takes on a very special almost mystical presence, seeming "to float" just above the ground bathed in the pool of light.

The church and manor of Chilbolton have always been associated with Winchester, first the Minster and later the Cathedral, to whom they were given by King Athelstan, the grandson of Alfred the Great... certainly a church is recorded here in the Domesday Book. Architectural experts say that the basic structure of what we see today is of a 14th century date, when the north and south aisles were added and much of the original nave disappeared. The chancel is earlier [13th century] and the tower and porch much later [19th century]. I was intrigued to discover that the former east window of the chancel is now in the west wall. The move was made in 1893, when it was decided to fit some new lancet windows in the east wall, as would have been there when it was originally built. I believe that the fine quality of the old east window tracery deserved rather better Victorian stained glass.

As you step inside St. Mary's you enter "centre stage" in the south aisle, between curtains of an heraldic pattern in blue and gold... very dramatic! Similar curtains shield the unused doors in the north aisle and in chancel where they complement a lovely blue carpet. This chancel has an atmosphere quite distinct from the nave, not least because of the Millennium "sculpture"[it only weighs 1lb.] by David Begbie symbolising 'The Risen Christ', invisibly suspended from the roof. It is best viewed from the nave, where it is visible high above the delicate wooden tracery of the 15th century screen. Behind a tasteful modern altar hangs an intricately carved and hinged reredos; the absence of detail on the two side panels gave me the feeling it was an "unfinished symphony". Returning to the nave there is a remarkably fine late 16th century pulpit, and standing here the full effect of the hundred or more newly stitched kneelers, creates a kaleidoscopic feast of colour as they rest in their pews.

Clearly there were separate altars at one time in both the north and south aisles, for the original piscinae are still to be seen. At the east end of the north aisle carved on a lintel over a doorway, is itemised the restoration work carried out in 1893, above it is a "window opening" for some of the organ pipes. In the south aisle a fine new Millennium Book contrasts 'World Events' and 'Events in Chilbolton' through the ages... very appropriate for this church where so many different ages and architectural materials have been blended to the glory of The Creator.

CHILWORTH
St. Denys

No clouds, no vapours intervene but the gay, the open scene
Does the face of nature show, In all the hues of Heaven's bow.

JOHN DYER 1700 - 1758

This little church high on a hill above Chilworth Old Village was built in 1812. Peter Serle Esq., provided the entire finance but it was not until 1849 that his gift was recorded on a plaque in the porch. The tower at the west end incorporates this entrance porch, and once supported a fine steeple, as is shown in some watercolours inside. In several places there appear to be "blind" single lancet windows, which seem unusual... the only other external features to note are the stone pinnacles to the eastern buttresses.

The charm of this church is within. The first thing that I noticed was the font on my right, it was certainly of Norman workmanship but apparently at some time had had the top half sliced off. It had much in common with other Test Valley fonts [those at Leckford, Goodworth Clatford and Kings Somborne for example] and around its base someone had recently placed four pretty little vases of wild flowers.

On the west wall are two boards, each recording gifts for the poor of the parish; to provide bread, clothing and medical aid. Nearby is a photograph of St. Denys' pair of 12th century bells reputedly the <u>oldest</u> in Southern England, and therefore very precious. In a glass case on the wall are the original clappers, removed from use to prevent the chance of damage to them. At the crossing,

the north transept accommodates the attractive organ and the south transept still has pews and chairs... both once had their own fireplaces. The sanctuary is defined by a narrow oak rail supported on a series of delicate Gothic arches in wrought iron, with two hinged gates in the centre. Above the altar the stained glass in the east window is late 20th century and depicts Mary with the child Jesus; Christ the Saviour; Christ the King, and St. John; above, the three tracery lights show the badges of Winchester, Canterbury and St. Denys. As always, the latter is shown holding his severed head, emblematic of his death as a martyr [he was the first Bishop of Paris in the 3rd century]. Either side of the window are Gothic arches, within which are written The Lord's Prayer and The Creed; beneath, are ten more arches for The Ten Commandments.

The greatest glory of this building, is its intricately panelled and vaulted ceiling painted in a deep shade of turquoise, with every boss, every corbel, from which the vaulting springs, highlighted in shining silver. The mirror images of the decorative Gothic arches do in fact link and entwine within the whole elaborate design, to form more distinctive arch shapes at the end of the nave, and over the entrance to the sanctuary. In this church there are indeed *all the hues in Heavens bow*!

48

CRAMPMOOR
St. Swithin

'The wonderful thing about saints is that they were human. They lost their tempers, scolded God, were egotistical or testy or impatient in their turns, made mistakes and regretted them. Still they went on doggedly blundering towards heaven'.

PHYLLIS McGINLEY   1915 - 1978

St Swithin was an important Bishop of Winchester in the ninth century, when that town was the capital of Wessex. He was chosen by King Egbert [802 - 839] to be his chaplain and tutor to his son, Ethelwulf. When he succeeded his father he appointed Swithin to be Bishop, in 852. Swithin died in 862 and according to his wishes was buried <u>outside</u> the Minster in Winchester. 120 years later it was decided to move his remains <u>into</u> the Minster. On the day chosen [15th July] it rained so hard that the ceremony had to be postponed. Perhaps it subsequently turned out to be 'a bad summer' and it felt like "forty days"! In such a way does folklore evolve.

St. Swithun's Crampmoor, is a "daughter church" of Romsey Abbey situated to the east of the town. Almost continuous traffic now flows along the main road to Winchester on the church's north side, and another busy local route inhibits access on the west side, however there is a convenient carpark at the back of the church. We were interested to see an early photograph of St. Swithin's as it was in 1896, showing clearly the rural nature of its environment at that time.

The building started life in 1858, as a school <u>and</u> a church, the funds being raised by three Victorian ladies, Mrs. Feltham, Mrs. Suckling and Mrs. Rolfe. Thus the nave fulfilled a dual function as a schoolroom, and the headmistress lived in the attached cottage... part of the cottage remains in use today as a kitchen and a meeting room. When a new school was built at Woodley in 1927, the <u>church</u> layout was made permanent.

Just inside the door is a neat alabaster font supported on four slender oak columns rising from a cross-shaped base. On the opposite wall is a most elaborate triptych, comprising twelve different classical religious paintings. It is in fact a high-class Victorian copy [by the Arundel Society], of the original one by Hubrecht dated 1432, and completed later by Jan Van Eyck. This one used to hang in the Romsey Vicarage until donated to St.Swithun's by Canon Norris in about 1960... it is truly remarkable. The Millennium Book being prepared by the parish, tells the chequered history of the original, [now in the town of Ghent]... a story of theft, loss and recovery lasting five centuries.

The nave is furnished with about 50 delightful beech chairs with plaited rush seats. The east end apse has four lancet style windows, and the altar, the pulpit and the priest's stall are all in polished light wood. At the west end is a model of this church made in 1935, and hanging on the north wall is a finely stitched representation of The Last Supper. Both these items were made by parishioners.

49

EAST DEAN
St Winfrid

England, with all thy faults, I love thee still...
...My country! and, while yet a nook is left
Where English minds and manners may be found,
Shall be constrain'd to love thee.

WILLIAM COWPER 1731 - 1800

The dedication of this church is to St.Winfrid, sometimes spelled Wynfryth, and more widely known as St. Boniface. He was born in Crediton in Devon in about 674 and was educated in Exeter and at Nursling Abbey near Southampton, where he was ordained at the age of thirty. He resisted attempts to persuade him to become the Abbot at Nursling and went on to devote himself to the evangelisation of the homeland of his Saxon forebears. He was eventually martyred there, at Dokkum in Friesland [now northern Holland] in 754, probably by Viking raiders. The bible with which he tried to ward off the attack still exists with the sword cuts on it, in the monastery he founded at Fulda in Germany in 744. His successful work in other parts of Central Europe, earned him his place in history as Papal Legate for Germany and Archbishop of Mainz in 745, which post he resigned after eight years, in order to continue with his evangelistic work.

This little church's dedication to him is not so surprising, since it lies on the natural route from Salisbury to Nursling via Romsey; firstly along the Dun River valley, and thence along the valley of the River Test to Nursling... I expect he knew this route very well. Sadly, Nursling Abbey was demolished by the Danes in 878 and seems never to have been rebuilt, much to the disappointment of German tourists who come to this country seeking their Christian heritage.

Driving along the road between Lockerley and West Dean it is very easy to miss this very interesting church, however quite recently some kind person has permitted the creation of a convenient carpark in a field alongside, with a new signpost and a safer access to the church. The main picture shows the church from the south side on one of those warm, but not too warm, summer afternoons when after your visit you might dream of taking tea in someone's garden.

The main entrance door on the north side is thought to be at least 600 years old and repays close inspection before you venture to open it. As can be seen opposite, over the top of the door itself is an amazing lintel which is shaped like a yoke. Inside St. Winfrid's enfolds you in a warm embrace, the grey ship's timbers of the wonderful roof and gallery, and the whitewashed walls have a freshness and a friendliness as of a favourite aunt's drawing-room. For the Millennium further "comforts" have been fashioned by clever hands; every pew bench has now a beautifully coloured swathe of "rag-rugging" upon which to sit, and a variation in the technique has produced kneelers of equal expertise, and with a new carpet for the aisle... well, it seems to welcome you as an honoured guest.

The little gallery at the west end repays a close look, for mounted on one of the supports, in a neat wrought iron holder [once perhaps for an extra-large candle] reposes... an iron cannonball! The curtained vestry is under the gallery too, and just in front is a small table where may be found a pamphlet on this church's history and a visitors book. A glance at some of the entries in the book, seemed to indicate to me that it had been used in the not too distant past, as a means of communication between a modern Romeo and Juliet, though hardly secret!

Apart from the lancet east window all others are square shaped diamond-paned clear glass, except for the west wall where above the square window is a circular one, presumably to give extra light in the gallery. Except for a reading light over the lectern I did not notice any other electric lights at all. It was to save on the expense of candles that winter evensong services were customarily held in mid-afternoon in most churches throughout the 19th century. I presume therefore that this factor still has a bearing upon the timing of services in St. Winfrid's to this day?

EAST TYTHERLEY
St. Peter

Full many a glorious morning have I seen
Flatter the mountain-tops with sovereign eye,
Kissing with golden face the meadows green
Gilding pale streams with Heavenly alchemy.
WILLIAM SHAKESPEARE 1564 - 1616

The upper photograph accompanying these words was indeed taken, as I'm sure can be seen quite easily, on just one such "Shakespearean" morning. The dawn mists are dispersing in the background and the top of the steeple is *flattered ... with sovereign eye* as are *the meadows green*. It comes close to perfection to be up and about at such an hour of the day, recalling for me memories of childhood summer holidays, when any adventure <u>before</u> breakfast added a very special ingredient to one's life.

My visit to this charming church was every bit an "adventure" in its own way. I admit to returning on several occasions and reaping a different reward each time. It lies in a park-land setting with some magnificent trees for company... the giant redwood 'Wellingtonia', around which the church drive circles, competes in height with the steeple, and without doubt will exceed it one day. There are also mature cedars in the fields nearby, evidence of the former estate of Denys Rolle [1725 - 1797].

The church has a medieval core of nave and chancel, though almost restored out of sight since so much Victorian attention has been lavished upon it! In the same photograph can be seen the unusual positioning of the transept tower and its somewhat hat-like shingled spire... very individual, and added in 1898. The entrance is just beside the tower and once inside there is a lot to see. If you first look up to the roof you may be reminded immediately of that magnificent double-arch in Wells Cathedral, in the exact way the main roof supports follow that same pattern.

Next your eye will inevitably be caught by the more than life-size mural of St. Peter, filling the whole space of the blocked north transept arch, which was originally open to where the bell-ringers stood. On a matt gold background, St. Peter is depicted in a plain brown monks habit, walking bare-foot towards you, arms outstretched in greeting. It was the gift of Hugh and Anne Dalgety on the occasion of their leaving the Lockerley Estate, and was executed by one of their friends, Jonathan Trowell in 1983. It is painted in oils on board and fills the whole space of the arch. Forming the base of the work, which is otherwise unframed, is written 'TU ES PETRUS ET TIBI DABO CLAVES REGNI CAELORUM'... this translated of course means, 'You are Peter and to you I will give the keys of the kingdom of heaven'. In my opinion the painting deserves to be more widely known... I believe it is worth coming a long way to see.

The very large single lancet window in the west wall is a fine stained glass memorial to a great benefactor of this and the neighbouring church of Lockerley... Frederick G. Dalgety Esq. In the south transept another stained glass window is his own, and his children's, memorial to his wife Blanche, who died aged only forty-six in 1886.

The chancel is quite special, in spite of the restoration of 1863 there is an ancient authenticity about it. The original archway of about 1250, and the careful re-use of some exquisite stained glass of about the same date in the rebuilt lancet windows, creates an atmosphere of tranquility and reverence. The theme of the blind arcading behind the altar is picked up in a separate "minature version" reredos above and behind the actual altar. This has a cross at its centre, and the whole effect is very much in harmony with its carpeted surroundings, and is given a wonderful softness by a display of tastefully arranged flowers on a pedestal at one side.

Before leaving I'm sure you will notice the attractive stone pulpit, and against the west wall, the panelling and the Gifford Memorial, repositioned here when the south transept was built. Since the first edition of this book was published, the knight's helmet of the Gifford family, which used to be above the entrance has been stolen.

EAST WELLOW
St. Margaret

Tell them in England if they ask
What brought us to these wars,
To this plateau beneath the night's
Grave manifold of stars.

It was not fraud or foolishness,
Glory, revenge, or pay;
We came because our open eyes
Could see no other way.

The Volunteer.   C. DAY. LEWIS 1904 - 1972

Although these words obviously were not written with the Crimean War in mind, they focus on the theme of self-sacrifice in a higher cause, with which St. Margaret's will ever be associated through the world-wide renown of Florence Nightingale, who lived in the parish as a child and who is buried here.

An annual service of remembrance and thanksgiving is held in this church, on the second Sunday in May, to commemorate her life and work, followed by a short wreath-laying at her memorial in the churchyard. Prominent among those who attend are the representatives of Nursing Associations from around the world, not least the President of the Royal College of Nursing and nurses from the armed services. On her memorial there is no name... just the initials F.N. as can be seen opposite.

There is, of course, a constant stream of visitors throughout the year, who having negotiated the narrow lanes of the final mile, are rewarded with all that one would wish to find in such a setting. The building is almost entirely of the 13th century with a later south aisle, and has an interior unique within Test Valley for the expanse and the quality of its original wall paintings, one of which in the chancel depicts the martyrdom of St. Thomas of Canterbury. The intimacy of its lovingly-groomed interior, where on our most recent visit every windowsill, every point of focus, was decorated with flowers of blue, purple, and white, as if for a flower festival, is difficult to describe adequately. It was easy to want to extend ones stay... to sit and just to be still here for a while, and forget the urgency of the world outside. We noticed one particular windowsill devoted to memorabilia of Florence herself, as real as if on a dresser in her own home. In contrast on the west wall is a formal print purporting to show Florence Nightingale at Scutari military hospital, which was clearly done to commemorate her achievments... an interesting "outline drawing" explains the identities of some of those in the picture, including the artist himself!

The fine font is a memorial to Rev'd. Empson, who died in 1883, and the east window of 1858 is in memory of Emily Empson, presumably his wife. The sanctuary is small and intimate with a St. Margaret window in the north wall and a St. Margaret figure beautifully applied to the blue curtain over the priest's door on the other side. The blue theme is also the basis for all the lovely kneelers; whose subjects varied from Emmanuel College, to Wessex Heartbeat, to Flanders Poppies etc. "Lording it" over all these at the front of the nave, was a superb pulpit with an octagonal tester, and opposite is a fine organ of 1927.

This church is not a shrine, it is an affirmation of those qualities in men and women, who *could see no other way* than to affirm their faith by "doing something"... one of whom on a particular occasion happened to be a young lady, named Florence after the city where she was born on 12th May 1820. She died in London on 13th August 1910, having been honoured during her lifetime by many countries. No honour was more deserved than the Order of Merit given to her by her Sovereign in 1907 [she was the first woman to be so honoured]. In accordance with her wishes, an official offer of burial in Westminister Abbey was refused by her relatives; her own choice was to be laid to rest here in the Hampshire countryside that she loved, close to her former family home of Embley Park.

ENHAM ALAMEIN
St. George

God of our fathers, known of old, Lord of our far flung battle-line, beneath whose aweful hand we hold, dominion over palm and pine... Lord God of Hosts, be with us yet... Lest we forget, ... Lest we forget.

Recessional   RUDYARD KIPLING   1865 - 1936

A mile or so north of Andover on the road to Newbury was once Kings Enham, or Enham Regis, a manor in its own right since at least 1443, but by the start of the 20th century it had become divided into three or four large private estates. Here in 1918, it was decided that land should be acquired for a settlement for disabled servicemen, and the resulting Enham Village was officially opened on 29th October 1919. In the quiet Hampshire countryside the veterans of the Great War recovered their poise and health, learnt new skills, learnt to cope with their disabilites and to contribute further to society. Another contribution to the amenites of the new community, was a chapel constructed on land near the centre of the village and very appropriately dedicated to St. George.

When in 1945 the residents of Egypt gave the British Government £225,000 in grateful thanks for the victory at the Battle of El Alamein, it was decided to use the money to expand the facilities of Enham Village to cater for the needs of a second generation of disabled servicemen, and to include the word Alamein. A veteran of that battle, the Rev'd. Leslie Pettifer was appointed to the adjoining parish of Knights Enham in 1969, and it became his earnest desire to have a permanent memorial in the village to his World War II comrades.

Hence the little church we see today... it may seem modest from the outside but to enter it, is to enter into a shrine dedicated to a precise moment in our history. It is most beautifully and tastefully furnished, every single item has a story to tell, and all around are the shield badges of the units who fought in the campaign. At the north end of the nave is the memorial chapel with three stained glass windows showing the badges of The Mediterranean Fleet, The Western Desert Air Force and The Eighth Army, on the wall above are the Corps and Divisional signs arranged in order of battle as at 22.00 hours on 23rd October 1942. In his account of the Second World War, Sir Winston Churchill wrote the following most appropriate words... 'It may almost be said, before Alamein we never had a victory. After Alamein, we never had a defeat'. What better reason could there be for the construction of this church, which was dedicated on St. George's Day 1974 by Rt. Rev'd. Colin James, Bishop of Basingstoke. The woodwork, produced in Enham's workshops by the comrades the fallen, reflects the warmth of fellowship among servicemen in general, both in adversity and in conquest. We, who have inherited the future for which they fought, should ever be grateful for places like this. In Kiplings words above... *Lest we forget... Lest we forget.*

FACCOMBE
St. Barnabas

...the thoughts by England given, her sights, her sounds, dreams happy as her day;
and laughter learnt of friends, and gentleness, in hearts at peace, under an English heaven.
The Soldier   RUPERT BROOKE   1887 - 1915

We hope you may agree with us, that our photograph of St. Barnabas epitomises some of the thoughts so wonderfully expressed by Rupert Brooke... a place where hearts can be, *at peace under an English heaven.*

Faccombe Church stands 753 feet above sea-level, and we know of none higher in Southern England, excluding the West Country. Here the light pours in from all angles, and the winds sweep the skies into an ever-changing tapestry of moving clouds, creating the perfect backdrop to a church of classic form. Yet it was not always here, for it replaced, only in 1866, the derelict St. Michael's Church in Netherton in the valley below.

The landscaping around the church invites you to wander around, for the grass is always immaculately mown. The roses by the lychgate are preceeded in the spring by a host of daffodils on the bank opposite, but whatever the season do not dwell too long before going inside. The first thing you will notice, I'm quite sure, is the font. The informative pamphlet for visitors tells a fascinating story about it, which I will leave for your investigation... suffice to say that it is very old, I know of only one or two that may be older in Test Valley.

Under the west tower is the vestry, within which on the south side there is a facility for playing the three bells called 'stationary chiming'. The bells are dated 1530, 1655 and 1987. Also in the vestry is a plaque recording the completion and restoration of the tower in 1897 by Mrs. Everett, the wife of the then rector.

At the western end of the nave among the memorial tablets on the walls retrieved from the old church, are those on either side of the entrance door in memory of Alice Reade [died 1598], and Anne Reade [died 1624], both of great interest. One other little plaque which we found stated that, 'Electric light was installed by parishioners as a thank-offering for peace', dated September 1938. Exactly one year later of course, the Second World War started!

At the east end of the church, the absence of a chancel at first seems quite strange, [it had to be taken down in 1963]. The effect is minimised by a carefully designed screen of oak panelling, which frames the sanctuary and altar... it also incorporates a pulpit. It was the gift of Mrs. Butler-Henderson in 1953. The east window, is a memorial by Rev'd. Everett to his wife Ann Jane mentioned earlier. In the centre, Christ the King is surrounded by angels, and on either side are St. Michael and St. Barnabas, patron saints of the former church down in the valley and this, its replacement.

If after spiritual refreshment, you need the other sort, we can recommend the inn just around the corner!

FYFIELD
St. Nicholas

God made the country, and man made the town.
What wonder then that health and virtue, gifts
That can alone make sweet the bitter draught
That life holds out to all, should most abound
And least be threaten'd in the fields and groves?

WILLIAM COWPER 1731 - 1800

If you think that Fyfield sounds a bit like "five fields" you wouldn't be too far from the truth. One of the earliest names of the area was Fifhidon or Fifhide... literally "Five Hides" as we would understand it today. A "hide" is thought to have been an area of land capable of sustaining a household... more than just a field.

The present day village of Fyfield possesses a most charming little church. It is accessible by car, but far, far better it is to walk there if you can, either across the fields from the Weyhill to Thruxton road, or to stroll down the short "green lane" through the wonderful avenue of beeches that leads from the village street. If you have some time to spare, you may like to try the first route, though there are a couple of stiles to be negotiated. On this route, you will find as you cross the first field, that the church is not immediately visible from the footpath, but once you enter the water-meadows of the second field it soon comes into view, peeping out from behind a couple of large ash trees at the end of the path. I trust you will find it to be, as in the verse above, a place of health and virtue,... and appreciate as the writer does, being in the fields and groves.

It is a fairly "private" sort of churchyard within a neat rustic fence, where the wild flowers of spring, mingle comfortably with the posies of remembrance on the graves. A little wooden gate opens on to a gravel path curving up to the door, but why not first rest awhile on the thoughtfully placed bench, and enjoy the tranquil setting, before entering the church's peaceful interior? Perhaps allow the bird-song and the lambs [in season] to divert your mind to countryside thoughts. Hopefully, you will not be disturbed by the occasional aircraft making its final approach into Thruxton Airfield, just out of sight to the west.

Had it not been for a devoted rector of the early 19th century, Rev'd. G.W. Smyth, there would probably be nothing at all for us to see today. The records show that he practically restored the whole church, and refurnished it,

in the years 1846 and 1847. He completed the renovations by constructing the porch with its boxed-in benches in 1851. There is a memorial to him in the church, and to his wife Mary, who was the daughter of the well-known Heath family of Andover.

Inside St. Nicholas', there are some fine stained glass windows. We particularly liked the one in the north wall of the nave, which is one of two in Test Valley representing Faith Hope and Charity, and which is a copy of a portion of a much larger window designed by Sir Joshua Reynolds in 1778 for New College Oxford. It is known as the 'Tapp' window since it was presented in 1914 by the Tapp family of Westminster, whose ancestors lived around here during the entire 18th century. The east and west windows complement eachother nicely, the former is a rood group and the latter depicts The Ascension. There is a fine war memorial on the south wall, resplendent with the newly re-painted badges of all the allies in the First World War, namely Belgium, France, Italy, Japan, Portugal, Serbia and U.S.A. with the United Kingdom in the centre. Its restorer was churchwarden Lindsey Smith. This impressive stone tablet was another gift of the Tapp family, designed by Sir Ernest George R.A. and sculpted by W.S. Frith of Chelsea.

On the south side of the chancel there is a window depicting St. Nicholas, and a memorial to Rev'd. Henry White, who was the rector here between 1762 and 1789. He was the brother of Gilbert White of Selborne. It was he, who enlarged the rectory to establish a school for the sons of some of his acquaintants, [this was a common practice in the late 18th century, when parents "with means" perceived the need to educate their sons for the professions and business, rather than just for politics and leisure]. Henry White's grandson was the architect William White, who built the churches at both Smannell and Hatherden, and entirely reconstructed St. Mary, Longstock; all are mentioned later in this book.

GOODWORTH CLATFORD
St. Peter

A multiplicity of bells,
A changing cadence, rich and deep
Swung from those pinnacles on high
To fill the trees and flood the sky
And rock the sailing clouds to sleep.

Church of England Thoughts
Sir JOHN BETJEMAN 1906 - 1984

If you feel like a short walk before visiting <u>this</u> church, I suggest you park your car in Green Meadow Lane and take the footpath across the fields towards the sound of the bells, it is the sort of experience, in which you can imagine Sir John Betjeman absolutely revelling. During the summer the copse of poplar trees alongside the path will inevitably rustle its pretence of a shower of rain, which hopefully the morning sunlight will emphatically deny as you stroll along. By the time you reach the mown field you can see the source of the bells... the ancient tower and spire of St. Peter's.

As with Bullington, the manor of 'Godorde' was the property of Wherwell Abbey until the Dissolution of the Monasteries in the years after 1538, thereafter the 'advowson' [the right to appoint the holder of the benefice, or parish] was held by the Lord of the Manor of Wherwell... only in 1959 was this right transferred to the Bishop of Winchester, when the parish was combined with Upper Clatford, and now it is linked also with Abbotts Ann.

On the weekday when we visited St. Peter's, the eight bells were being rung by a team of visiting ringers who had already visited other churches in this area. The 'changes' they rang as we rather self-consciously wandered around the interior of the church, seem to fit the architectural experience, where the changing methods of construction and style were clearly visible, and carefully recorded for any visitor to follow. The Norman ancestry of this church is very obvious and it is known that around 1190 works of enlargement were carried out.

Historians now say that it was just before this time, towards the end of the reign of Henry II, that the Normans and the Saxons began to regard themselves as English, and as Sir Arthur Bryant put it... 'As the nation grew in wealth and civilisation, more and more public business was left to local men of worth, rich enough to take communal responsibility under the Crown, yet not strong enough to act without it.' This is also the time of Richard I and the European crusades to regain Christian control of The Holy Land... significant financial enterprises. The inference is, that there was money enough for church projects of all kinds, as well as to find Richard's enormous ransom of 100,000 marks, to free him from imprisonment in Germany when he was on his way home from the war.

The interior of St. Peter's consists of a Norman nave having some delightfully carved capitals to many of the columns, with two aisles and an enlarged chancel added around the end of the 12th century; all have been rebuilt from time to time in the intervening years. In the south aisle the original 15th century windows have been re-used. Although the structure of the chancel is also original, the windows here seem very clearly to show evidence of Victorian replacement. The north aisle has a most interesting dis-symmetrical roof profile and is the brighter of the two aisles, having only one memorial stained glass window to a member of the Iremonger family, whereas the south aisle has all four utilised for that purpose and the chancel too!

The extent to which these Lords of the Manor have been benefactors of St. Peter's is at once apparent even before close inspection of the stained glass; for on arrival the carving on the lychgate [1890] reveals that it also is another such memorial, and the porch likewise. The fact that Rev'd. Thomas Lascelles Iremonger was for 47 years the rector here during the 19th century has had, presumably, no small bearing on the matter.

The architecture of this lovely church is complemented by its art, as you will no doubt discover for yourself. Also in this category, is the ancient font just inside the door on the left as you enter, itself artistically ornamented with great skill... another Test Valley treasure.

GRATELEY
St. Leonard

...And thou my mind aspire to higher things, Grow rich on that which never taketh rust. Whatever fades, but fading pleasure brings.

Sir PHILIP SIDNEY 1554 - 1586

Occasionally, due to historical factors one finds that a village church has become remote from the modern village centre, but not here in Grateley. The little circuit of roads forming the nucleus of the village, encompasses the church, the school and the Manor Farm, and around its periphery, mainly on the eastern side, are the houses, the village store and the pub.

St. Leonard's Church is of Norman origin, but in the 13th century the nave and the chancel were rebuilt and the tower added on to the west end of the church, which later had a spire. The spire was severely damaged by gales in 1781, 1795 and 1818 and eventually was removed. The entrance to the church leads from the farmyard, then a short path brings you to the porch, which dates from 1738. Apart from this and the refacing of the external walls during the 19th century, we see the church more or less as it was 750 years ago.

Inside, its real "claim to fame" must be the relatively small fragments of stained glass that once belonged to Salisbury Cathedral. Since 1981 they have been incorporated into the south-east window of the nave. There is one complete diamond-shaped panel within the quatrefoil which shows the martyrdom of St. Stephen [the first Christian martyr], complete with an explanatory text in Latin and two other sections in the tops of the two windows beneath. They are undoubtedly some of the oldest examples of stained glass in England and <u>may</u> have been manufactured here. [Earlier examples <u>do</u> exist, notably in the cathedrals of Canterbury and York, but are known to have originated in France]. According to the style of this glass, it is said by experts that it... 'must have come from the east end of the cathedral, which was ready to receive glass from 1225 onwards'. St. Leonard's church history, tells us that these fragments were rescued by William Benson Earle in 1787 following the wholesale destruction of Salisbury Cathedral's medieval glass by the architect James Wyatt. Whatever the final opinion as to their country of origin, they are certainly worth viewing.

Mr. Earle was a real benefactor of this church for he also built the porch and installed a clock, replaced by the present one in 1858... it seems the benefactors keep coming as the centuries pass. Here, unusually perched among the rafters of the nave, is a carved and colourful holy rood of impressive proportions. It was erected in 1934 as a memorial to William Boucher, by his widow and his children. In the tower are two bells [dated 1583] and were no doubt installed during the time when it was ordered that bells should be used as a warning of a Spanish invasion.

HATHERDEN
Christ Church

Through leafless boughs the sharp winds blow, and all the earth lies dread and
drear; and yet God's love is not withdrawn; His life within the keen air breathes;
SAMUEL LONGFELLOW 1819 - 1892

This is the sister church to Christ Church, Smannell, built in the same year [1857] by the same architect William White. William was the son of Francis Henry White of Abbotts Ann, and the grandson of Rev'd. Henry White of Fyfield.

The choice of a winter scene for this church was deliberate, for as the photograph shows, the roof-line has been changed and the new metal roof is less conspicuous when covered with snow! However, we must be grateful that the church is still here, metal roof or not, for during the early hours of the 8th July 1975 the church was struck by lightning and the building gutted by a fierce fire, which left only the walls still standing. The Hancock Bible was rescued by the incumbent, the Rev'd. Collins, which though not old [1971], has a most beautiful illuminated inscription inside to record the circumstances of its dedication. The bible rests today on a new lectern, which was a 'renovation gift' from Vernham Dean Parish. The arising of the new church from the ashes of the old is a story in itself. The tribute book that records the various gifts of the congregation and others, is displayed for all to see, just inside the door.

Similarities with Smannell are very evident as one might expect... the nave-and-apse design, the brickwork, and the windows etc., but be ready for something of a shock as you open the door and go inside, for the building has been divided since the fire, and in the vestibule there are reminders of it all around... the memorial book has photographs from the local paper and beneath the west window is the charred font cover. The west wall still has the war memorial brasses in place and apparently unimpaired by the devastation.

Beyond the partition, one enters a totally late 20th century almost "drawing-room" environment. The walls are panelled in light oak with plaster above, and the whole floor is carpeted in a pleasant shade of green. The church now possesses a very interesting ceramic font supported on a matching plinth, which has a small interior cup; beside it on a small table is also a matching candle-holder. We have not seen anything like it before. It was made at Aldermaston Potteries and is handpainted in a leaf design using shades of sea-green.

The altar reminded us of the one in St. George's, Enham Alamein, so may well have been made locally. The wooden altar rail has wrought-iron and brass fittings, which match the lectern... clearly the opportunity created by the fire, was taken "in both hands" and the result is a most pleasant environment for worship and prayer.

HOUGHTON
All Saints

We are a garden walled around
Chosen, and made peculiar ground,
A little spot enclosed by grace
Out of the world's wide wilderness.

ISAAC WATTS 1674 - 1748

South of Stockbridge on the minor road to Mottisfont, you will come to The Boot Inn in Houghton. Opposite is the War Memorial and winding gently uphill away from it, is Church Lane, a quiet cul-de-sac at the very end of which, on the right, beautifully positioned in the shade of some tall trees is All Saints Church. Most definitely for us, *a little spot enclosed by grace*, in the words above of a poet who is most famous for that hymn 'Our God our help in ages past', [later changed by John Wesley to, 'O God our help in ages past', which is what we sing today]. Another verse of that same hymn begins with the words 'Under the shadow of Thy wing, Thy saints have dwelt secure...' We feel sure that looking at the accompanying photograph, you will feel as we did on our visit, that here indeed is a secure place for "all saints".

This most picturesque of churches, with the sweeping falls of its lovely tiled roof, and its shingled tower and spire, provide a welcome today as they have done in years past, to the indulgent visitor or the more purposeful pilgrim. Indeed, there is much evidence of such pilgrims, where they have scratched their crosses on one or other of the columns inside, and on the door posts. It is presumed that they were on their way to or from the shrine of St. Swithin at Winchester, or possibly they were on the longer pilgrimage to that of St. Thomas a Becket in Canterbury.

The massive interior columns help to provide a date for the earliest part of this building, which is of the late 12th century. Cut right through the one at the east end of the south aisle, and through the corner of the wall at the end of the north aisle, are hagioscopes [or squints]. The most likely rationale for their construction, is thought to have been to permit the congregation in the side aisles, to see the activites at the main altar... they were only discovered seventy years ago. It must be remembered that chancels used to be screened from the nave in most pre-reformation churches, and reserved only for priests.

As soon as one is inside All Saints, one cannot fail to be aware of the four massive wooden posts dating from the 15th century, which form the supporting framework for the bell tower... very similar to the structure in Mottisfont Church. Just on the left of the door is the children's area in memory of L. E .Rowan Bentall. If you stand near to the late 12th century font, which has a fine octagonal cover by Sir Giles Gilbert Scott, and look eastwards, you will see very obvious differences to the right and left of you. Arches have been formed in the north nave wall, which stem not from columns as on the south side, but out of the wall itself. A detailed church guide notes among other matters of interest, the position of a piscina in the wall of the north aisle, hinting at the existence of a separate chapel there, before the aisle was lengthened to its present dimensions. In a niche at the back of the aisle, which seems to have been once a north door, stand the modern sculptured figures of a mother and child entitled 'HES-ED' by Lucy Wynne [1996], a cousin of the incumbent at the time. The concept has similarities with that of the Millennium window in All Saints Church at Smannell... a mother and son in a "timeless grouping".

The main east window in the chancel and the east window in the north aisle, contain the only stained glass in the church; the former is a rood group of about 1875 and the latter, dated 1892, seems to be quite obviously a representation of Christ's healing of 'Blind Bartimeus'. Whilst in the chancel do inspect the beautiful kneelers at the altar rail. The fact that into each emblem is stitched both gold and silver wire threads, will give you some idea of the quality of the embroidery... likewise the altar frontal was worth coming a long way to see. On the occasion of a visit during Lent, it was a gold cross on a background shading from claret to navy-blue, and on an earlier visit we had seen the remarkable 'Tree of Life' depiction [shown opposite], presented in June 1994 by the Sarum Embroiders in memory of their founder, Mollie Collins who was a parishioner.

HURSTBOURNE TARRANT
St. Peter

*But somewhere deep down, I have a dim hope... that when the mists begin to lift and
the poplars to shiver and the cock-pheasants crow in the beech-woods, the little
bourn will awake and open her eyes and find again the exiles that she thought were
gone for good, and me too perhaps, kneeling beside her as of old, and watching...'*

Where The Bright Waters Meet.

H. PLUNKET GREENE, 1865 - 1936

We may imagine self-imposed *exiles* returning after some years away from the Bourne Valley and perhaps choosing to return along the route now familiar to so many, [that of the Test Way Footpath] as it slices diagonally downwards across the slope of Doles Copse towards the village below. If it were to be the early spring of the year, the bluebells would be casting their familiar mantle under the new feathery, meltingly green leaves of the beeches, and through the growing canopy there would be tantalising glimpses down below of the village itself, the school, the bourn and St. Peter's Church, old familiar landmarks now visible... now not... until finally out in the open and clear of the tree-line, there they all would be, exactly as depicted in the new Millennium window inside the church... "Home at last" they might say.

From our imaginary vantage point, St. Peter's draws us to itself in its lovely setting on the opposite slope slightly above the valley floor, and our travellers would easily see its lychgate and smart gravel path leading up to the door. This entrance, dated about 1180 is contemporary with the oldest part of the church, and will itself have "seen" many at the beginning of their lives happily carried through its portal, as they were brought as babes for Christening, probably at one or other of the two [possibly Saxon] fonts possessed by St. Peter's. No doubt years later and more sadly, it will have "noted" each villager's departure, as their lifespan was completed and they were laid to rest in the lovely churchyard.

Inside, the layout of the church is still as was created in the early years of the 13th century with its impressive Norman columns, though it is known that its foundation pre-dates the Norman invasion. Further enlargements were carried out about 1450, including the formation of the clerestory and a new nave roof. At the rear of the nave the massive beams that support the tower form a natural

chamber for the bellringers. Fixed high above them overlooking the nave are displayed the Royal Arms of George III, and on the wall beside the ringers are the 18th century Benefactors Boards, one kindly donating the interest on Turnpike Securities to provide books and tracts for the parish.

The two panes of the western-most window in the north aisle, now have the delightful engravings by Tracey Sheppard of Winchester, celebrating the recent Millennium. Ancient art is also here, in the shape of medieval wall paintings... it is well worth reading the explanations for both, thoughtfully provided for the visitor. We are sure the north aisle must once have had its own altar... the south still has. Near to the latter are the two War Memorial Brasses and the War Memorial Window, and on a little table the 'Book of Kneelers'. This is a work of art in itself, and records all who were involved with the making or sponsoring of the 126 kneelers now hanging beneath the pew shelves... we hope like us you will enjoy their amazing variety.

The chancel [its interior is shown opposite] is a Victorian re-build, entered by climbing four steps and passing between two gates. It contains a 15th century east window with stained glass of 1934. This is of the apostle brothers, James and John, and Peter and Andrew; each identified with an appropriate biblical quotation. The communion rail has turned balusters and fleur-de-lis decoration and is dated as being 1604-1621. It is a relatively recent gift to the church [1969].

The windows in the upper photograph show how the work of stonemasons became ever more skilled through the centuries, and are convenient examples of the windows of different periods. The one on the far left is a simple lancet of about 1200, with its "next-door neighbour" being some 300 years later; the others are of the intervening periods.

KIMPTON
St. Peter and St. Paul

Far from the madding crowd's ignoble strife
Their sober wishes never yearned to stray;
Along the cool sequester'd vale of life
They kept the noiseless tenor of their way.

Elegy Written in a Country Churchyard
THOMAS GRAY 1716 - 1771

We have a book about Great Eversden, a village in Cambridgeshire compiled by our sister-in-law Lindi Wood, called 'Quiet Lanes and Orchard Ends'. The title she chose to describe her village contains that certain essence of meaning with which we can all relate, perhaps allowing our imagination to range among a myriad of memories of our childhood and youth, and those in particular, that first awakened our love of the English countryside.

Here in Kimpton one such picture memory can find its manifestation. The village church of St. Peter and St. Paul lies at the end of one such 'quiet lane', overlooked would you believe, by an 'orchard end' as can be seen opposite. Almost as if it had been especially sited, shyly, to hide behind the wonderful apple blossom on a warm May morning, trying to pretend it was not there.

Archaeologists have discovered evidence of community life in this quiet corner of what now we call Hampshire going back to 2000 B.C., and we know for certain that for at least 800 years [and probably more] the yeomen of England... indeed the bowmen of England in their time, have been baptised and buried, worked, rested and worshipped here in this church. The very special brass memorial [dated 1522] to Robert Thornborough and his two wives, Alyse and Anne, and their nine children in the north transept sets the scene for us. Later, from 1750 for over a hundred years, there is memorial evidence of the Foyle family too, some of whom seem to have been Rectors of the parish.

The quiet green lane already mentioned, by which we walk to this church is slightly raised above the level of the surrounding fields, because there are times when the winter-bourn makes its presence very obvious and access would otherwise require Wellington boots. From the exterior one can quite easily see how over the centuries the church gradually evolved into its present cruciform shape. One major work to the original, the rebuilding of the south aisle, is carefully recorded on the exterior wall near the entrance with a date of 1702 and the names of the churchwardens at the time. The rather smart and decorative brick and flint tower, portrays its date of 1837 by the lancet-shaped openings on the south face. One imagines that it might be a replacement for something of an earlier date, for its corner turret is reminiscent of those on the only other similar towers at Longparish and Barton Stacey, but which are three hundred years older. Real lancet windows adorn the chancel, which is dated to 1220. The transepts were added about one hundred years later and at the same time the chancel extended.

Inside, this church has some nice little surprises for the visitor. The south aisle so carefully preserved in 1702, is actually only wide enough for a couple of chairs, so must qualify for the title of the narrowest in the borough. If as you walk around you glance back towards the western end, you may detect a rather subtle "blue-ish light" filtering in through the tower west window. We assumed it was something to do with the type of glazing. It may not have been intentional but none-the-less we found it created a very pleasant atmosphere.

Over the beautifully adorned little altar in the north transept, there were two ikons of the type usually associated with the Eastern Orthodox Christian Church, and on a wall at the back of the church, there is a fine framed example of calligraphy, describing the division in 1925 of the old Winchester Diocese into the three existing dioceses of Winchester, Portsmouth and Guildford.

We had the pleasure of once escorting a blind lady of eighty-nine to be confirmed in this church; on that occasion and on our most recent visit, we could sense that to the villagers of today, St. Peter's and St. Paul's Church is as precious and important as it ever was.

Here as much as anywhere, that well-known verse at the top of this page from Gray's epic poem, seems to fit so well.

KINGS SOMBORNE
St. Peter and St. Paul

The day becomes more solemn and serene
When noon is past... there is a harmony
In autumn, and a lustre in its sky,
Which through the summer is not heard or seen
As if it could not be, as if it had not been.

Hymn to Intellectual Beauty

P. B. SHELLEY 1792 - 1822

This is a church to take at your leisure, perhaps on an autumn afternoon as the poet describes above, with the late sun warming the shingled tower in its glow, just as it was when the exterior photograph was taken. On such occasions churches have a way of introducing people to one another. My arrival was almost coincident with that of the piano-tuner, and during my stay the organist also came in. He it was, who very kindly was able to "unmask" for me the originals of the two brasses of the 14th century stewards of John of Gaunt. Although this is <u>Kings</u> Somborne, its history is closely connected with the third of Edward III's sons, John of Ghent, or Gaunt. In common with his other brothers, who were created the first ever English dukes [of Cornwall, Clarence and York], he was created Duke of Lancaster in 1362 and built a palace here. He spent very little time in England, mostly serving with his brother The Black Prince fighting the French in Gascony, and between 1386 and 1389 he tried unsuccessfully to persue a claim to the throne of Castile in Spain... how romantic, if this connection was found to be linked to the first part of the village name! The truth is no doubt more prosaic.

The church was extensively restored in 1886; a record of the event can be seen carved into the masonry of the first column of the north aisle. Almost all the windows in this aisle are old ones re-used, and at the east end a fine 14th century one now forms the focus of a little chapel [the subject of the second photograph] dedicated to The Virgin Mary. An old embattlemented corbel protects a small statue of her, which stands in a little niche in the wall.

The chancel once had a beautiful late Jacobean rail [now positioned in the south aisle], which was 'highly regarded by Pevsner' so the church guide tells us... and I can see why, for it seems to be a unique transition piece, fashioned just when the classical theme was about to erupt onto the English "stage". The chancel has two low arches,

which once connected with two chapels on either side; one has become part of the north aisle and the other houses the organ. Standing in the chancel, if not before, the visitor becomes aware of the multiplicity of new needlework in this church. Evidence of great expertise is everywhere around you. Every conceivable surface seems to have been cushioned and decorated. Hanging over the priest's door are beautiful curtains, with almost life-size figures of St. Peter and St. Paul on them. Special cushions were done for the choir stalls to celebrate the Millennium; one a village panorama, the other, 'A thousand ages in Thy sight' depicting varying means of transport. There are one hundred and fifty new hassocks, and a banner showing the names of all those married since 1993, which also includes in most cases a piece of the material of the brides' dresses.

As far as stained glass is concerned, there is an interesting contrast to be observed in the east and west windows, both are memorials to different owners of the same estate, Compton Manor. The Edwards' east window of 1885, has as its subject The Ascension with the eleven disciples in attendance, whereas the Sopwith west window is much more modern [1996], and shows the Archangel Michael defeating the Devil in personal combat. This for me, evokes a close association with the aerial combats fought in both world wars by pilots flying aircraft designed by Sir Tommy Sopwith and his companies. High in the roof above the window is the belfry. I had noticed outside on a board that a Millennium Appeal had raised money for the removal, re-tuning and re-hanging of the six bells... their green and white sallies were looped neatly to one side. What I was not quite so prepared for as I was leaving, was my encounter with a parishioner at the church gate, whose first words to me were "Do you believe in God?" I had no hesitation in answering in the affirmative, and I hope our subsequent conversation, though short, was beneficial.

KNIGHTS ENHAM
St. Michael and All Angels

The winter evening holds her peace and makes a crystal pause,
Frozen are the streams of light silent about their source.

C. DAY. LEWIS   1904 - 1972

Although the accompanying photograph is taken in winter, you can happily arrive at this very special church at any season of the year and be enriched by the rustic tranquility of its setting. In the spring the churchyard has its carpets of snowdrops... in the summer the shielding limes and beech trees throw a protective shade over its ancient walls, and in the autumn you will not need us to describe the colours, as the time comes for the same trees to gently drop their leaves on the sacred ground, and *evening holds her peace.*

The newly gravelled path to the church door picks its way through a veritable "guard of honour" of table tombs, but pause here just long enough to see clearly defined on the south wall the shapes of the arches of a former, grander church in whose aisle you almost tread.

As you enter the neat little porch, you may find perhaps that the old 17th century door ahead of you requires a little "gentle persuasion" to open, but this may just give you enough of a pause to read the message on it. Once inside, the entrance to the chancel is interesting, being in fact a group of three wooden arches resting on a cross beam. This feature is beautifully decorated at times of major festivals and candle-light sevices... on the wall above is a board bearing the Royal Arms of Charles II. Hanging from the roof in front of it, is a lovely 18th

century brass candelabra and looking beyond it, can be seen a richly coloured stained glass Victorian east window, with St. Michael in the centre flanked by two of the other archangels, St. Gabriel and St. Raphael.

The memorials and hatchments on the south wall of the nave might give the impression of your having intruded upon a family chapel, certainly a slice of their history and our country's history is here, recorded in a style which could easily grace a cathedral. On the charity boards nearby, you will no doubt notice, that the concerns of the local English squire for his estate workers and their families in 1789, were in stark contrast to the situation in France that year, where a revolution was in progress. Other texts painted on the walls remind us of days when a Book of Common Prayer was beyond the means of many of the worshippers and the bible was frequently chained to its lectern.

Not chained, but kept in the Cathedral Treasury in Winchester, are the silver chalice and paten belonging to this church, which are of exceptional rarity, having been made during the time of Cromwell; one, the gift of David Kingsmill in 1654, and the other that of the Rector Thomas Brathwayte himself in 1655... examples of the affection, in which this church was held at that difficult time, and is still held today.

LECKFORD
St. Nicholas

I often wished that I had clear, for life, six hundred pounds a year, a
handsome house to lodge a friend, a river at my garden's end, a terrace walk, and
half a rood of land, set out to plant a wood.   JONATHAN SWIFT 1667 - 1745.

To speak of Leckford today is immediately to think of the name John Lewis. If the words quoted above had been part of his education at Westminister School 100 years ago, it could be said that he achieved the aims expressed, here on the Leckford Estate. This he acquired after the death of his father in 1928. His success in business and his far-reaching ideas of "partnership" with his entire workforce, were put into practice here as much as in any of the famous stores, which still bear his name today. When he moved to Longstock House in 1946, his former *handsome house* in the village of Leckford itself, did indeed *lodge a friend* and continues to do so to this day [the "friends" in this case being the staff of the partnership]. There is indeed *a terrace walk and a river at my garden's end* <u>more</u> than that... a water-garden of great reputation and beauty, which is open to the public at various times throughout the summer. *Of land set out to plant a wood*, there is also ample evidence. In fact he planted an arboretum in the grounds of his new home.

The village of Leckford is on the main road from Andover to Stockbridge and if you travel too quickly, you can be through it perhaps before noticing the church of St. Nicholas tucked away behind its yew tree. The church, in common with Mottisfont and Knights Enham and

others, is of a typical medieval village style, and additionally has a sundial above the priest's door in the south wall of the chancel, which you are bound to notice as you walk up the path to the porch.

Internally the west end of the nave is dominated by the posts of the bell tower but hugging the sides are some very old benches crudely converted to pews. Here also stands the Norman font, almost an exact twin of that in St. Peter's Goodworth Clatford, probably slightly earlier, because its low relief Norman arcading does not vary at all. To the east the nave is full of box pews, which are overlooked by a beautifully carved 16th century tester pulpit, which looks to have been adapted to fit the narrow wall space. More adaptation was probably needed to accommodate the remarkable choir and sanctuary seats, which originated from an Italian monastery and were presented in 1923. The old stone altar, discarded during the Reformation by decree, is now back in place. It would probably have been removed during the reign of Edward VI, when it was deemed more correct for altars to be replaced by tables; more properly to reflect the scene of The Last Supper. The stained glass east window of 1874 shows the three Marys of the New Testament... all other windows are diamond-paned clear glass.

LINKENHOLT
St. Peter

*I have felt a presence that disturbs me with the joy of elevated thoughts; a
sense sublime of something, far more deeply interfused, whose dwelling is the light of
setting suns, and the round ocean and the living air and the blue sky.*

WILLIAM WORDSWORTH 1770 - 1850

The quintessential Englishness of the situation of St. Peter's Church here in Linkenholt, is like something out of a novel. The church stands just across the road from the cricket ground, there is a little matching schoolhouse next to it, and to the right and left are the farm and the manor house. *The joy of elevated thoughts* could easily be a batsman's "six" into the churchyard, but I think we may be sure that Wordsworth had in his mind, *something far more deeply interfused* and looking at the photograph, will we hope bring those ideas to mind... certainly *the blue sky* is in abundance.

The church was built in 1871, on a new site just a couple of hundred yards from the old one, which had become 'ruinous'. Records only show definite evidence of a church in the village after about 1320, but the manor had been owned by the church since 1081, having been passed to the Abbot and Convent of St. Peter, Gloucester, by Ernulf de Hesting a vassal of William the Conqueror. How appropriate it was therefore, when to celebrate the church's refurbishment in January 1999, a former Bishop of Gloucester, Rt. Rev'd. John Yates, was invited to the special service.

The smart lychgate invites entry, as does the sweeping path across the neat lawns leading to the porch. Before entering however, do notice the lancet window on the left, which is decorated with twenty-five 'shepherds crowns' [fossilised sea-urchins often found in the fields around the village]... the smallest window on the north side is similarly decorated. The shape, size and apparent age of this latter window gives it a Saxon feel, which together with the Norman arch of the doorway and the distinctive Norman font inside, [both known to have come from the former St. Peter's], must be evidence of a church building here at least 150 years earlier than the 14th century date we have above, and perhaps of another 150 years before that!

Inside, the west end of the nave is dominated, firstly by the two massive oak posts, which support the steeple, and secondly by the font already mentioned. This has the same style of embellishment as the one in St. Barnabas, Faccombe, but not to such a depth. The fine stained glass west window contains the figures of St. Michael and St. Gabriel, and the even more impressive south nave window, is a Faith, Hope and Charity window. Above the altar is an east window of three lancets, each of which depicts one component of a rood group. We hope you will appreciate your visit as much as we did, and be fascinated as we were, by other interesting archaeological items in a display case. What are they? You will have to visit to discover!

LITTLE SOMBORNE
All Saints

*The worst had not happened... it was as if the whole world was shaking
itself free of the burdens of the past and cladding itself everywhere in a white mantle
of churches.*

RALPH GLABER 1003.

These words by a Burgundian monk, written of his homeland in 1003, are I suspect, an equally appropriate description of England at the end of the <u>first</u> Millennium, and this little church is part of the evidence.

Of all the churches which are of Saxon origin within the boundaries of the Test Valley Borough, Little Somborne is unique. Often we are left with no more than a font or a window or, as in Romsey Abbey a Holy Rood sculpture, to remind us of our pre-Norman ecclesiastical heritage. Here, barely changed over the past 1000 years, not only can we see the actual size of the original marked out on the floor, but also the original window openings and even the actual one thousand-year-old plaster on the window splays.

The more confident use of stone for church building after the year 1000, in replacement for the former wooden structures, speaks of faith restored as well as the financial means. England was at this time a rich land... King Ethelred could afford to buy off the Viking invaders year after year, apparently meeting their ever more outrageous demands with relative equanimity and only occasional force. Since then, alongside the headwaters of the Sombourn, very little has happened to disturb the natural rhythms of rural life, and thus the tiny church retains much of its original form.

Finding this church will reward the visitor, coming upon it with a suddenness and a fulfilment that can illumine even the dullest day. The picture shows it as it was in March 1994, with the host of daffodils which surround it, bending to the gusty north-west wind. Inside you will find all is peace and you will have no difficulty finding your "place", for this is where we all belong, as much a part of history here, as in a great cathedral. Rest awhile and if in spring, listen to England slowly awakening to another year... what will you hear? Perhaps the birds in the trees that frame this little sacred plot; the wind as it sighs through the great yew tree outside or swirls around the 16th century bell turret tightly holding its solitary bell... merely 400 years old! Before you leave I expect you will wonder as I did, how that little Chicago-made organ found its way from the 'new world' to assist with the worship of the old?

Little wonder though, that Sir Tommy Sopwith who lived nearby, should choose his last resting place to be here; modestly on his headstone are just the words, 'Pioneer Aviator'. He, who with others, first placed in the hands of men in the 20th century, the ability to become the conquerors of the daunting sky, lies with the first inhabitants of this hamlet, for whom even the Battle of Hastings was a future event!

LOCKERLEY
St. John the Evangelist

The cloud-capped towers, the gorgeous palaces,
The solemn temples, the great globe itself,
Yea, all which it inhabit, shall dissolve
And, like this insubstantial pageant faded
Leave not a rack behind.

The Tempest.
WILLIAM SHAKESPEARE 1564 - 1616

A hundred and fifteen years ago you would have seen here a church, which to all intents and purposes was exactly the same as those that still exist at Mottisfont, Knights Enham or Leckford; yet to adapt some of Shakespeare's words above, it has dissolved and left *not a rack behind*. Happily we still have a cloud-capped spire, if not a tower in our photograph! The reasons for this situation are to be found in the generosity of one man, Frederick Gonnerman Dalgety, who bore the whole cost of this new church built in 1890.

Mr. Dalgety became the founder of an international company. He sailed from England to Australia in 1833 at the age of sixteen to seek his fortune, which he proceeded then to make by providing supplies to the sheep farmers and shipping their wool to England. It was not without risk, but he had a reputation for loyalty and integrity in his business affairs, and in the end became an exceedingly rich man. He returned to England in 1854, married in 1855, and proceeded to raise a family of thirteen children. He brought extensive estates in East Tytherley, Lockerley and East Dean and built Lockerley Hall in the "Sandringham" style between 1868 and 1870. He became High Sheriff of Hampshire in 1877.

This church is not only his legacy, but is his own memorial, for there are two attractive stained glass windows in the chancel to his memory, and the east window depicting The Ascension is one he himself commissioned in memory of his father, who apparently was a Lieutenant in the Royal Irish Fusiliers. In the century or more since its consecration in 1890, the church has become as much a part of the village as was its predecessor as can be seen immediately on entering. The vaste array of embroidered kneelers is presented as if for exhibition on the book-shelf of each alternate pew, too many to count, but fascinating in their variety. I saw a butterfly, a horse, a smiling face, one depicting the old Lockerley Church, one to the memory of

an RAF officer, one to the village Silver Band etc., all adding a splash of wonderful colour to the interior. Elsewhere, there was recorded that in 1991 the village children had planted daffodil bulbs in the churchyard, to mark where the foundations of the old church had stood... no doubt the ancient yew tree nearby appreciates their company in the spring.

The elegant wooden screen that shields the organ in the north transept, and all the other woodwork, is of Kauri Pine from the Dalgety family estates in New Zealand and is of course contemporary with the other fittings; among which are the really impressive brass rail to the sanctuary and the finely carved stone pulpit, not surprisingly very similar to the one in East Tytherley... presumably they were given at much the same time by the same donor. Behind the altar is a marble reredos of The Last Supper. The south transept is entirely occupied by the 'children's corner'. Here is one of the tiniest lancet windows in the whole of Test Valley; clearly a relic of the previous church, or of even an earlier one! It is now a memorial to Bertha Cattle, the village schoolmistress between 1883 and 1919. Beneath it, is a miniature altar and on the wall alongside an "illuminated" copy of The Lord's Prayer... not to be missed!

Fixed to the wall below the clear glass of the large west window is a display cabinet holding memorabilia of Frederick Luke V.C., who was born in West Tytherley in 1895 and lived in Lockerley. Driver Luke and his comrade Driver Drain, and their commanding officer of the 37th Battery R.F.A., Major D. Reynolds, all won their V.C.s at Le Cateau in France in August 1914, when they volunteered to try to recapture two guns, which were under fire from the enemy just 100 yards away. All three survived the attempt and one gun was recovered. Frederick Luke joined the R.A.F. Regiment in the Second World War and died in Glasgow in 1983.

LONGPARISH
St. Nicholas

God's eyes shall be open, and His ears intending on this house night and day; that the asker in it shall receive, the seeker shall find, the ringer or knocker shall enter.

Book of St. Bartholomew's Church LONDON 1135.

It is possible to park quite close to this church, but to our mind a more attractive approach is to take the Test Way Footpath from the hamlet of Forton. The level path across the wide water-meadow cannot be mistaken and the superb 16th century tower "dressed" in chequer work of alternate flint and stone, beckons you forward, until you find beneath a lime tree, the recently restored western lychgate into the churchyard. This is a place to pause and rest awhile even on a clear winter's day; the more so in summer when enjoying the tree's shade.

A 19th century porch protects the original 12th century doorway, but it was not until our departure that we noticed on the door itself, and read, the entire passage from which the above text comes. It is salutary in these modern times to find such faith expressed, and beneficial too. It is said that the 'greatest temptation is to doubt'... how true that is for all of us. There is no doubt however that this church retains a special place in the hearts of the village it was built so long ago to serve. No doubt you will notice on entering, the light permanently glowing behind the cross on the altar, it gives the feeling of "presence". Having *entered*, you are invited to *seek* and *find* something more in *this house*. A prayer desk is positioned discreetly in the central aisle and you are invited to leave your written petitions on it as others have done, or kneel and offer

them in your own way... you will not feel alone in so doing.

A new roof was put on in 1853 and the old clerestory windows were "lost". This event, combined with the fact that all the other windows but two are of stained glass, has created a very gentle and diffused interior light. The east window depicting a Nativity scene is an amalgamation of two designs of Sir Edwin Burne-Jones, executed by Morris and Co. after his death. In the north aisle, is the memorial window to Major Lanoe George Hawker V.C., D.S.O., of No. 6 Squadron Royal Flying Corps, with its evocative and detailed scene of a First World War aerodrome in France. Major Hawker was awarded the Victoria Cross on 25 July 1915, when he managed to destroy three enemy aircraft during the course of one sortie. Sadly, he was shot down himself and killed near Bapaume, France in November 1916. Other memorials nearby showed that the Hawker family had lived for several generations in Longparish House.

Outside, you may hear the sound of aircraft of a different century. It would not be surprising if in these circumstances, you were minded to think of all those who fought and died in the air in both World Wars, and like us, recall those words found on many a memorial, 'FOR YOUR TOMORROW, WE GAVE OUR TODAY'.

LONGSTOCK
St. Mary

O happiness enjoy'd but of a few, and if possess'd, as soon decay'd and done
As is the morning's silver-melting dew, against the golden splendour of the sun.

WILLIAM SHAKESPEARE 1564 - 1616.

The Longstock estate and village, together with that of Leckford across the river, forms part of the holding of the John Lewis Partnership. It is a village of rare charm in a most beautiful part of the Test Valley.

If you are feeling energetic, then the finest walking route to the village, is that which takes the old chalk road from Danebury Hill slowly descending down into the valley. Often on your left you will see buzzards soaring along the ridge, and if you are very lucky, as we were on one occasion, you may see Britain's smallest bird... the goldcrest, fluttering from one hedgerow to the next.

Longstock extends itself along the western side of the valley on the back road from Stockbridge to Fullerton; at its centre stands St. Mary's on a bank and within a hundred yards in either direction, are the pub, the smart modern village hall, and the war memorial.

St. Mary's in our photograph is bathed in some of Shakespeare's *golden splendour of the sun*, but no doubt before very long the *morning's silver-melting dew*, will have *decay'd and done*. In our imagination therefore let us enter the churchyard under that imposing lychgate built in 1907, carved upon the entrance of which, are the positive words 'There shall be one flock and one shepherd'. After passing between the old yew tree and its oriental neighbour, an unusual ginkgo tree, the path brings us to the porch and thus into the church itself. This was re-constructed by William White in 1880 on the site of a much earlier edifice and he incorporated some of its original features into the design. [Fortunately for historians, two faded photographs of that building still remain on the vestry wall]. Immediately to the left stands the 14th century font, behind which is a little stained glass window on whose ledge stand a crucifix and two delicately designed brass candlesticks. Two crown candelabra of the same but more elaborate style, hang in the nave and the same design theme is carried into the choir stalls.

The chancel is entered through a carved wooden screen which is in harmony with the adjacent choir stalls. Other beautiful oak panelling is fixed to the walls around the altar. The east window crucifixion scene was made for St. Mary's in Munich in 1882, but we urge you also to admire the nativity scene in the memorial window to Joshua East, in the chancel's south-east corner; in particular the exquisite artistry of each of the four halos around the heads of the principal figures. Finally look above you, this is a William White roof and no mistake, complete with accompanying angels; sadly two have been "modified", one to accomodate the organ pipes, the other the chancel arch.

MICHELMERSH
St. Mary

Therefore my lords, omit no happy hour
That may give furtherance to our expedition,
For we have now no thought in us but France...
...therefore let our preparations for these wars
Be soon collected, and let all things be thought upon,
That may with reasonable swiftness add
More feathers to our wings.

Henry The Fifth
WILLIAM SHAKESPEARE 1564 - 1616

Glebe Meadow, Wheables, Priest Hay, Shingland and Bell Rope are just a few of the names of the fields that surround St. Mary's Church, names which have been commonplace for hundreds of years in this ancient village of Michelmersh and in which King Henry V's army gathered waiting for a favourable wind to take them from Southampton to France. A copy of the village charter granted by King Ethelred The Unready dated 985 is held in the British Museum. The king, 'Aethelred the Redeless', [his name in this older form can mean both 'unready' or 'lacking in counsel'] was the one who tried to buy off the Norse invaders and eventually fled to France in 1013, leaving his son Edmund in charge. Only briefly it must be said did Edmund restore English fortunes, before the Danish Canute took over the kingdom from him in 1016, and married his widowed mother one year later.

At first sight St. Mary's immediately catches one's attention by virtue of its tower that stands apart from the church. We know of only one other similar wooden church tower, and that is St. Augustine, Brookland, on Romney Marsh in Kent. It is thought that St. Mary's tower was probably erected in the time of Elizabeth I, in response to a decree that all churches should have bells to warn of any invasion. As previously surmised, we believe that most of the little bell-turrets seen on our Test Valley village churches were put up at the same time for the same reason. For financial reasons they could not match this imposing edifice, which is indicative of the local importance of Michelmersh. As so often in our researches, we were indebted to an informative pamphlet available for visitors, for the additional information that the cladding is of oak and has to be replaced every eighty years... apparently the next time will be in about 2050!

It is easy to be beguiled by the tower and the whole setting of this church and to fail to appreciate fully some of its other wonderful features... the porch for instance, the beautiful silver-grey wood of which, speaks of a "polishing" by countless south-westerly gales and of a scorching by Hampshire summer suns. As we step inside, we enter the south aisle with the font to our left in a sort of alcove dominated by the memorial plaque to Sir William Ogle [later Viscount Ogle of Caterlough in Ireland], who commanded the Royalist garrison of Winchester Castle during the Civil War. The font is remarkable for the quality of the four carved stone heads at each corner, thought to be evidence of restoration work around 1500. Nearby on the wall is a time chart of the Second Millennium, enabling an easy cross-reference between events in the village and the wider world beyond, since 985. To the right of the door [date 1798] are two clear glass windows, clear except for the newly engraved names of all the incumbents of the parish since records began... perhaps another Millennium commemoration.

There is very little stained glass in St. Mary's. The main east window is in a typical late Victorian style and is a memorial to the eighty-third Bishop of Winchester. More modest is the glass in the two small lancets above the west door, again Victorian, showing a pattern of the emblems of the four countries of the United Kingdom. The south-west window of the chancel, installed in 1988, is a commemoration of 1000 years of parish history.

Here in the chancel also, lies a marvellous stone effigy of a knight in armour thought to be Sir Geoffrey de Canterton, whose family were known to live in the parish during the 14th century. I feel sure he would have felt very much at home in the presence one hundred years later of the Duke of Gloucester, who reviewed Henry V's troops here on 16th July 1415 prior to their embarkation for France, and their ultimate destiny at Agincourt. We may even imagine the Duke encouraging his men with words not unlike those above imagined by Shakespeare.

MIDDLE WALLOP
St. Michael

What was, what might have been, fighter and bomber
The tilting sky, tense moves and counterings:
Those who outlived that legendary summer;
Those who went down, its sunlight on their wings
And you unborn then, what will you make of it...
This shadow-play of battles long ago?
Be sure of this: they pushed to the uttermost limit
Their luck, skill, nerve... And they were young like you.

' Battle of Britain' Film Premier Programme. 16th September 1969.

C. DAY. LEWIS 1904 - 1972

Opposite, is the Station Church at Middle Wallop on a day in early May 1996. This was the Sector Operations Room of No.10 Group R.A.F. during the Battle of Britain in 1940. Inside this very building those familiar war film scenes of WAAF plotters moving the details of enemy raids across the operations table, were enacted on a daily basis. From here squadrons were directed on to their targets... here it was known first how the battle progressed; here was known first the names of those who would not return to fly again the next day. The urgency of those times, had caused the original plan for Middle Wallop to be altered from a bomber station to a fighter station. There was no time to build a proper operations room in a reinforced concrete bunker, only the "temporary building" hurriedly constructed of wood that we see still intact today. The station came under attack several times during the war, and still today you can see, when the hangar doors are closed at night and the lights are on inside, the holes where the bullets went through them. There are some other original war time buildings, which still show evidence of the camouflage with which they were painted all those years ago, and there are still concrete "pill-boxes" around the airfield perimeter.

This building [St. Michael's] was dedicated as a church in 1953 by the then Chaplain-in-Chief of the R.A.F. The Rev'd. A. Giles, perhaps on the same occasion [18th October] that he dedicated the Bell Tower in the foreground of the upper photograph, which is in memory of all those, service and civilian, who lost their lives between 1939 and 1945 serving on this station.

Protected from the elements by the porchway is a fine 1920's style, oak entrance door with a small inset panel of stained glass showing St. Christopher, but why not St. Michael you may ask? The answer is that the door formerly belonged to the station chapel of R.A.F. Andover. Inside, it is still so easy to visualise the wartime scene, but the fitted royal blue carpet and the altar at the north end immediately bring one back to the present day. The oak altar rails and other furniture were given in memory of Gp.Capt. and Mrs. Grece and define the sanctuary [further details about them are included in the Over Wallop narrative]. Behind the altar hangs a large wooden cross decorated at the time of my visit by four large fronds of palm, and surmounted by a "Crown of Thorns" made by the children of the Sunday School. In the east and west corners of the sanctuary hang two groups of flags... as one might expect, they are the Union Flag and flags of the units associated with the Army Air Corps. Just inside the door on the left is an 'army' font... small, octagonal, made of portland stone, which is supported on a frame of four oak pillars. Close by are five steps leading up to where the Sector Controller and his staff would have been positioned during the war; now it is the choir and organ gallery. On the front of this balcony are fixed military shields and squadron memorials. On the opposite wall are some fine examples of calligraphy... framed copies of the R.E.M.E. and Army Air Corps collects.

The church is lit by tasteful modern groups of five hanging lights. During an entirely <u>candle-lit</u> Midnight Service on Christmas Eve 2000, the gallery lights suddenly came on, on their own, just as the chaplain lit a final candle and said the words "Jesus Christ the Light of the World, has entered the world". They could not be turned off until the main fuse was removed after the service! The circuitry was inspected later and found to have no fault... an amazing experience for those present, I suspect.

MONXTON
St. Mary

There is sweet music here that softer falls than petals from blown roses on the grass.
Here are cool mosses deep; and thro' the moss the ivies creep, and in the stream the
long-leaved flowers weep. ALFRED, LORD TENNYSON 1809 - 1892

Tennyson, writing the words above, could well have been seated in the garden of The Old Rectory next door to St.Mary's on a warm summer afternoon. It is also likely that he would have recognised another "music"... a sound like the lightest summer shower of rain, caused by the fluttering movement of leaves in the grove of poplars next to the churchyard, as they oscillate in an almost imperceptible breeze. The poet's *cool mosses* are here and *the ivies*, as is the stream in which *the long-leaved flowers weep.*

The manor of 'Ann de Bec' [now Monxton] as opposed to its neighbour of 'Ann de Port' [Amport], probably derives its name from its ownership by the monks of Bec, whose prior Lanfranc was appointed Archbishop of Canterbury by William the Conqueror. Alien priories were "suppressed" by Henry V in 1414, and later, in 1441 his son Henry VI gave the manor and the church to Kings College, Cambridge.

To find the church [Monxton's best-kept secret] from the centre of the village, you have to go over the little stone bridge spanning the stream, until you see on your right the First World War Memorial Gates leading to St. Mary's. The footpath winds around the boundary of the Old Rectory garden, and even when you feel the church has <u>got</u> to come into view, it still attempts to hide behind

a lovely yew tree. At first glance it looks the twin of Wherwell Church, but it was built two years earlier in 1854. The main difference is that inside, there are no aisles. The first thing that caught one's eye was a very nice framed watercolour of the church hanging on the west wall. In contrasting style at the other end of the church, forming part of the reredos behind the altar, we found a fine oil-painting of a subject very seldom seen, namely The Supper at Emmaus; this in turn was framed by two modern oil panels of a young lady... Mary, we assumed?

The chancel arch is Victorian, but springs from 12th century capitals, and is almost entirely covered in elaborate lettering. At the top is written 'God spake these words and said', and beneath on both sides are the commandments in an abbreviated form. There is a separate archway opening in the north side of the chancel wall, presumably to help the sound of the organ to be heard more easily. Here also, often stands a wonderful floral display. There was a brass plaque on the wall nearby to a lady named Alice Swayne, who died in 1599 at the amazing age of ninety-eight, if our calculations are correct! Another beautiful floral display was in the sanctuary, and high above all, a fine east window showing Christ in the centre, flanked by Mary and St.John in robes respectively of vivid blue and red.

MOTTISFONT
St. Andrew

O pastoral heart of England... like a psalm
Of green days telling with a quiet beat.

Sir A. QUILLER-COUCH 1863 - 1944

This lovely spot is certainly a *pastoral heart of England*, and was the same when the religious priory was founded here in 1201. In those days the little church of St. Andrew would have looked the poor relation to the magnificent building just across the road. Today they no longer have a complementary role in presenting the Christian Gospel, for a good part of the former priory [now known as The Abbey] has all but disappeared to the casual eye, and become a fine secular dwelling owned for the benefit of us all by The National Trust. The little church alone retains the spiritual mission to the community.

It was first built in Norman times, perhaps about a hundred years before the priory. Since no outer aisles were added in later centuries, the robust nave walls remain more or less as they were built. A central aisle tiled in alternate black and white tiles, now showing their age, leads forward to the impressive archway leading into the chancel. Here, there <u>have</u> been alterations, which are mostly of a 15th century date, with the windows reputedly having 'the finest collection of 15th century glass of any village church in the county'. On the south wall of the chancel is a memorial dated 1584, though we had to rely on the handy church history board for this information. In the nave, in what may have been a tomb recess on the south wall, is a striking wooden carving of 'praying hands' by the late Peter Martin, a parishioner. It was carved from timber removed from the belfry and is accompanied by that lovely prayer... 'Grant me the serenity to accept the things I cannot change...' etc., which is very well-known. On the same side of the nave just inside the door, is mounted a most interesting clock said to date from 1640-1670. It has a mechanism similar to the famous clock in Salisbury Cathedral, with some very impressive stone weights.

The sallies of the five bells were hooked conveniently out of harms way when we were there, but entering prior to a service when the bellringers are in position must be interesting to say the least! Perhaps that is when the south doorway is used.

From the churchyard the 'medieval village' form of this church is apparent, enlivened by the piebald effect where the rendering has been repaired. The windows on the south side are a fascinating "hotch-potch" of varying styles; basically they are double lancets, which have been adapted to taste as the centuries have passed. This little church no doubt gains visitors from its proximity to its well-known neighbour 'The Abbey', in whose beautiful grounds is the famous "font" or spring, from which the village takes its name.

NETHER WALLOP

St. Andrew

*....A treasure-house divine
Of peaceful years; a chronicle of heaven.*
WILLIAM WORDSWORTH 1770 - 1850

The approach to this beautifully preserved corner of Hampshire, wherein St. Andrew's Church "nestles" into the ground, cannot better be achieved than by strolling along the little lane that leads from The Five Bells public house... the church's presence comes upon you much like a well-loved friend suddenly appearing around a street corner. The carefully tended churchyard with its steep steps and path leading down to the western end [beside the pyramidal monument to a former village doctor], bids you to take care, but perhaps before descending, take advantage of a short rest at this vantage point by making use of the thoughtfully provided 'benches of remembrance'. From here one looks out across the valley towards the iron-age hillfort of Danebury, at least two thousand years older than the church below.

It is perhaps a little difficult to reconcile Wordsworth's words above, with the condition of England at the turn of the first Millennium when this church was built by Earl Godwin of Wessex, [the father of King Harold of 'Battle of Hastings' fame] in about 1016. Even as we consider the intervening years between then and now, we cannot fail but to be enfolded in the peacefulness of the scene which has hardly changed since then. Sited halfway down the slope above the level of the Wallop Brook, the church seems to sit on a natural terrace, looking down upon the roofs of the thatched cottages clustered around the stream below.

Externally, very little if anything overtly Saxon is visible, but to enter through the 14th century door is to walk back to that time, for above the chancel arch is an exceptional example of Saxon wall painting known as 'Christ in Majesty' attended by angels. Unfortunately this practically unique painting, was partially destroyed by the Normans when they extended the chancel, and widened the arch beneath it in about 1200. Later extensive rebuilding alterations, perhaps around 1420-1430 added their own individuality, including more wall paintings designed to teach "The Moralities"... art

historians are well provide for here!

The north door itself is old enough, but the doorway is even older and must have been repositioned when the aisles were added. On entering, one's immediate interest in the famous wall paintings should not divert attention from the north aisle. Here against the outer wall [and similarly in the south aisle] are probably the oldest benches or pews in the whole of Test Valley, they must be at least five hundred years old, we believe. No less remarkable are the eight new pews added in 1984, totally in sympathy with the old ones, and grouped to form a small chapel at the east end of the north aisle. Here they are overlooked by two stained glass windows, the one in the north wall entitled 'Suffer the little children to come unto me', is recorded as being given by the 'Sunday School children and others' at Easter 1909. The octagonal stone font at the west end of the nave has the same quotation around its rim and completes the wording with... 'and forbid them not, for of such is the kingdom of God'. The impressive brass-work design that decorates the font cover seems to be contemporary with other brass fittings in the church, notably the amazingly tall free-standing candelabra on either side of the altar. Our guess is that the 'others' mentioned above also gave this church all these gifts at about the same time. Incidentally, the east window of this north aisle [also dated 1909] is clearly of 'The Three Kings presenting their gifts to the infant Jesus'... but the composition seemed to include a fourth "king", or were we mistaken?

Under the tower is the ringing chamber for the six bells, and quite by chance it was our good fortune to visit the church one evening in April 1998 when the bell-ringers were practising. Their natural hospitality led them to offer to illuminate the chancel for us as we wandered around, and the resulting photograph of the interior was obtained. A depiction of what we hope, may be for you as it was for us, *a treasure-house divine of peaceful years; a chronicle of heaven.*

NORTH BADDESLEY
St. John the Baptist

Six centuries have gone
Since, one by one, these stones were laid
And in air's vacancy, this beauty made.
They who reared them their long rest have won;
Ours is now this heritage...
To guard, preserve, delight in, brood upon;
And in these transitory fragments scan
The immortal longings of the soul of Man.

WALTER de la MARE   1873 - 1956

Of course, one should not take the lines above too specifically. It certainly could be argued that this church is more than six centuries old, for it has a history going back to the Domesday Book, but apart from the walls of the nave, most of what is obvious today is of the 15th century or later, particularly the west end and the tower, which has its date emblazoned upon it. It is of the year 1674, and shows a very early use of brick in an ecclesiastical building. It is likely that the square stone foundations of the tower and the porch are from the former adjacent premises of the Knights Hospitallers of St. John of Jerusalem, "dissolved" in 1536, and granted by Henry VIII to Sir Thomas Seymour, brother of Queen Jane Seymour.

Ours is now this heritage... and this is a lovely example of the way in which recent generations have taken up the challenge enshrined in the words above. The porch shows evidence of the wear of centuries and signs of repairs during Victorian times. Within it, a pew weathered almost white and matching the beams above, provides a place to sit and appreciate the scent of the roses growing by the roadside gate. Once the intricacies of the locks have been solved, there remains just the iron lever attached to a huge bolt on the inside of the door to be slid to the left, and the door swings open on beautiful 17th century strap hinges. One can understand the need for the heavy blue velvet curtains on the inside of the door, for its planks have shrunk and light and air have free passage through numerous crevices!

This is by no means a large church, hence the need, as at Knights Enham near Andover, for an additional Church Centre nearer to the new building developments of the village. At the west end is a gallery for the choir and organist added in 1822 and reached by a "semi-spiral" staircase. The front of this gallery is enriched by some very fine modern linenfold panelling, and attached to it is a plaque dated 1660 with the Royal Arms of King Charles II, [coincidentally, Knights Enham possesses a similar one]. Apparently, this one was repainted in 1806, which could account for the addition of the symbols 'G 3', for George III. A very fine guide book entitled 'North Baddesley Church and Village' expounds a very plausible theory that the chancel screen inscribed 'T.F.[meaning Thomas Fleming] 1602' was originally in the church at North Stoneham. I have to say it looks fine in this position and is thought to be of contemporary date with the tester pulpit alongside it. On the other side of the nave is a remarkable iron-banded parish chest complete with a hollowed out piece of a tree-trunk for its lid... black with age.

On the north side of the chancel is a glass fronted cabinet, in which reposes a second edition of   The Authorised Version of the Bible dated 1620, and rather squeezed into the remaining available space is the medieval chest tomb of a Knight Hospitaller, and adjacent to it is a very fine, but rather large mural monument. The stained glass east window of 1923 has the crowned figures of Mary and the child Jesus in the centre, with St. John the Baptist and St. Swithin on either side. The boarded ceiling above is painted a sky-blue, with the supporting ribs in gold and red with heraldic shields at their bases... a beautiful example of restoration in 1987. If anything, the two cross beams of the nave are even more elaborate, with chamfered edges of glistening gold and designs of gold and green on the lower face, and gold and red on the sides... outstanding!

NURSLING
St. Boniface

The spacious firmament on high, with all the blue ethereal sky,
And spangled heavens, a shining frame, their great Original proclaim.

JOSEPH ADDISON 1672 - 1719

'Nursling Farm stands on high ground on the south of the road. In the fields nearly opposite, one of which is known as 'The Walls' is the site of the ancient Benedictine Monastery... destroyed by the Danes about 878...' This is an extract from The Victoria County History of Hampshire. More recently doubt has been expressed about the monastery's exact location. Certainly, the Saxon Wynfrith, or Winfrid, later to become known as St. Boniface, set out to convert his ancestors to Christianity from Nursling. It is entirely appropriate that this church should be dedicated to him. He was born in Crediton in Devon about 674; he was educated in Exeter and at Nursling Abbey where he was ordained in 704. He declined the position of Abbot when elected in 717 and decided to become a missionary. Although he failed to convert the Frisians of the North German coast at his first attempt, he had better success elsewhere in Germany and eventually was appointed by The Pope to be Archbishop of Mainz in 745. His work has been described as 'one of the most important acts of evangelisation in European history'. Later he resigned his high office to return to Friesland, where he died a martyr's death in 754.

St. Boniface's stands almost at the end of a real country lane, yet within sight and sound of the busy M.27 motorway, but that apart, the setting is a very lovely one for the churchyard contains a fine collection of different trees. In the entrance was quite the oldest ladder we have ever seen, providing means of access to the tower. Although the church is basically 14th century, with two massive beams of that time stretching across the whole twenty-five feet width of the nave, the pews and windows are clearly Victorian. The stained glass east window is dated 1902, and seems to depict Christ as 'Transfigured' in one panel and as 'Risen' in the other.

The west wall is decorated with two hatchments and in the centre is a little recess with a slightly pointed arch, into which a covered table has been fitted. Upon it, we noticed evidence of contacts with St. Boniface's Church in Lippstadt, Germany. Looking eastwards one's eye is drawn to the lovely 16th century pulpit and nearby, the bright green banner upon which the figure of St. Boniface stands with axe and tree-stump [illustrating a famous event in his life]. At the entrance to the chancel there is a fine brass lectern of about 1885, but it is within, that a real surprise awaits. Here is, presumably, a former memorial chapel now used as a vestry, containing the amazing full-size colourfully painted reclining effigies of Sir Richard and Lady Mill, and various other momentos... a veritable museum of parish history.

90

OVER WALLOP
St. Peter

I lingered round them, under that benign sky... listened to the soft wind breathing through the grass; and wondered how anyone could ever imagine unquiet slumbers for the sleepers in that quiet earth.   EMILY BRONTE 1818 - 1848

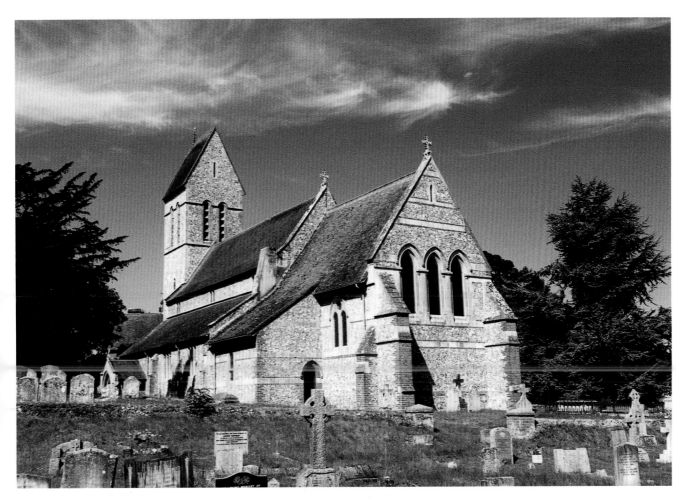

The vicarage and the church in Over Wallop have their own bridge over the Wallop Brook. Once crossed, we admit, we *lingered under a benign sky* and could not help but notice among *the sleepers in that quiet earth*, the group of military headstones on the left of the drive, among which are those of Sir Clement Harman [Lord Mayor of London in 1963-1964], and his wife. They chose to be buried here alongside their brother, daughter and son-in-law [Group Captain Grece, the Station Commander of Middle Wallop], all three of whom had died together in a flying accident on 12th July 1954.

The present church is mostly an elaborate Victorian rebuild [the original church was dated 1180], which was begun in 1864 and completed in 1874. It owes its existence to Rev'd. Henry Fellowes, a younger brother of the Earl of Portsmouth. The original windows, of differing architectural periods, were all re-used in the new walls; only those in the 15th century north aisle wall have remained in their original setting.

On entering, the unusual presence of a blue-painted plough, may catch your eye, and how appropriate we thought in this farming community. This plough, apart from its manufacture in modern material, was not so different in size and shape to the one in The Museum of the Iron Age in Andover, even though more than 2,500 years separate their use!

Close by, there is an elm display case, holding a facsimile of the Hampshire section of the Domesday Book, and two other tables, made by a parishioner. The capitals of the last two nave columns display four stone corbels from the old church, which seem to depict a King, a Queen, and possibly a Lord and his Lady, in medieval dress. The 15th century font positioned right in front of the tower vestry, has the heraldic arms of the Wallop family on one of its panels.

In the north aisle the accident victims mentioned previously are further commemorated, in what has become a memorial chapel of wider significance. Three standards now hang there, those of the British Legion, Royal Air Force and Glider Pilot Regiment, the latter placed here on Remembrance Day 1957 following the disbandment of the regiment on the previous 1st of September. However, the Victorian Gothic "tour de force" of this church, is the chancel with its very high archway. Across the front is an unusual wrought-iron screen with an integral wrought-iron pulpit, on the screen a cross and the keys of St. Peter are picked out in gold. High and imposing the chancel certainly is, and the same adjectives could apply to the candelabra in the sanctuary and the three lancets above.

PENTON MEWSEY
Holy Trinity

And this our life, exempt from public haunt, finds tongues in trees, books in the running brooks, sermons in stones and good in everything.

As You Like it   WILLIAM SHAKESPEARE 1564 - 1616

No more than a short stroll from The White Hart public house or the cricket ground, Holy Trinity Church stands in a secluded spot between the old rectory and what I assume was once a glebe meadow, over which there is an alternative access, and which becomes a sea of buttercups in the early summer. It was from this spot that the photograph was taken, permitting a good view of its little bell turret. Within, hang two bells which are said to have come from a Worcester foundry and be of a similar age to the church... if so, they are probably the oldest in Test Valley, <u>except</u> for those in St. Denys, Chilworth.

The pathway leading to the main entrance to Holy Trinity, is entered by a gate where a lantern on a slightly leaning post hangs among the branches of a magnolia... what better invitation could one need? Shielded by a yew, which has a circular seat around it, the late 19th century porch leads into a simple nave and chancel built originally between 1340 and 1350, on the site of an earlier church mentioned in the Domesday Book. Much restoration work was done in 1888, and after a fire in 1889, a new roof was also required, so much of what is visible is Victorian. One thing that is <u>not</u> 19th century is the ancient font, a feature of some size just inside the door, and it is a focus of beautiful decoration for all the major festivals, as is also

a special trellis framework, which can be fixed in the chancel arch. This I saw being used during my visit prior to Christmas 2001. I also noticed a very beautiful brass lectern, which seemed to be of the first years of the 20th century.

Apart from some remnants of medieval glass in the nave window on the south side, the only other stained glass is in the colourful west window, with a date of 1869 in its inscription. The little sanctus bell [of 1555] which hangs on the south wall of the chancel has had a very interesting and chequered history. The full story is told in Anthony Raper's, 'Andover... The Civil War and Interregnum', suffice it to say that it survived being secretly hidden in the vicarage garden wall, and was only rediscovered quite by chance in 1845.

Eight R.A.F. graves exist along the north boundary of the churchyard... among them, three of the five victims of a crash on Andover airfield, on 22nd of April 1919. Andover's connection with the R.A.F. has been an enduring one; the R.A.F. Staff College was opened at the airfield in 1922 and the station was granted the Freedom of the Borough in 1955. The town also had the honour of having a service aircraft named after it... many will remember hearing on news broadcasts, the words, 'An <u>Andover</u> of the Queen's Flight...etc'.

92

PLAITFORD
St. Peter

An English home... grey twilight poured on dewy pasture, dewy trees,
Softer than sleep... all things in order stored, a haunt of ancient Peace.

ALFRED, LORD TENNYSON 1809 - 1892

The words above seem to have been written for this church enfolded as it is, in a rather secret place as if to preserve it from the modern world... here indeed is *a haunt of ancient peace* of *dewy pasture, dewy trees.* The autumnal photograph shows off the richness of the ironstone quoins against the contrasting flint facing; also visible in the blocked 13th century south doorway.

The entrance is now on the north side and once within, I paused for a moment and just looked around me... to my right was a gallery filling the western third of the nave and reaching almost up to where I stood. In front, was the organ [by Boston of Winchester], and to my left was the rest of the nave, where the eye is taken immediately up to the steeply angled roof. This is embellished at intervals with painted mouldings in green and red which spring from a carved wooden frieze. Fixed at intervals, were small painted wooden shields depicting the badges of all the dioceses of Southern England at the time of rebuilding.

In the traditional place stood an oak pulpit and gleaming upon it, two single branch twisted brass candlesticks. A smart maroon carpet covered the whole of the chancel floor, whereas the sanctuary was decoratively tiled. Some real medieval tiles are preserved, inset into the back of the sedilia on the south wall. The entire east wall is curtained below the three stepped lancet windows, which hold the only stained glass in the church... St. Peter and St. Paul stand either side of 'The Good Shepherd'.

The west gallery is a charming and irresistible feature of St. Peter's, it is supported on three slender cast-iron pillars, and its panelled front is decorated in Gothic arches attractively painted. Beneath it, the space has a more informal feel; the font is here, and I noticed a very large Victorian copy of Pilgrim's Progress. Right at the back of the church fixed to the side walls, are two steel, arched panels, obviously 19th century, upon which are elaborately painted, The Lord's Prayer, The Creed and The Commandments. The staircase to the upper part of the gallery has recently been renewed, so I had no hesitation in ascending. Old benches stand on tiered platforms rather like in a stadium, and the whole area is back-lit from the window high in the west wall, [visible in the photograph]. Inside in the apex of the roof beneath the belfry, the triangular space displays an example of the Royal Arms dated 1980, and I thought I saw some remnants of medieval wall paintings on the side walls, half-hidden by the ends of the benches.

By the way, this is the only church in Test Valley, which is part of the Salisbury Diocese.

QUARLEY
St. Michael the Archangel

The Church's restoration
In eighteen-eighty-three,
Has left for contemplation
Not what there used to be.

Hymn
Sir JOHN BETJEMAN 1906 - 1984

As with many other Test Valley churches mentioned in the Domesday Book of 1086, it is thought likely that a Saxon church once existed here <u>before</u> that date, and there are some interesting features still visible that seem to confirm this, in spite of the major restoration works that were done between 1878 and 1882. I don't think John Betjeman had Quarley in mind when he wrote the poem quoted above, because the work here finished one year too soon, but we're close enough... and it's worth reading the rest of the poem I can assure you!

This church is another of that large category of those which amply reward the visitor, even though some might think that it lies rather "off the beaten track". However, it can be discovered easily, close to the country road that leads from Grateley through the village of Quarley and on towards Thruxton Airfield. It holds a rather special place in our journey through Test Valley, by virtue of its quite remarkable 'Venetian' east window of strongly classical design, on which an inscription reads, 'William Benson and Henry Hoare. AD. 1723'. Henry Hoare <u>senior</u> was building Stourhead at this time, one of the earliest Palladian buildings in England, and Mr. Benson was also the architect there. It so happened that Mr. Henry Hoare <u>junior</u> was Lord of the manor of Quarley in 1719, so this must account for Mr. Benson's involvement here with St. Michael's Church.

There could have been a Saxon window in the west wall above where the entrance door once used to be, and another [now filled in] next to the new entrance. If you look high up to the right of this door, the outline of stones set in a radial fashion, which once formed an arch over it, can easily be seen. Blocked up in the north wall is evidence of another very old window opening and a equally old doorway. Having walked round to the north side of the church to see this, one cannot fail to notice a most unusual belfry. It is little more than a roofed wooden structure surrounded by neat iron railings, in which the three bells are hung at ground level in the open air! The bells can be rung by using ropes which pass through the wall into the vestry. It is not often one can get so close to bells as this, particularly one of 13th century date... it is marked with a small black letter 'S' on the shoulder. The other two are dated 1636 and 1686, the first of which has the words 'Love God' on it, and the second, 'Ave Gracia'. In 1905 Henry Paulet, 16th Marquis of Winchester, paid for this bell to be recast and his name was added to the original inscription.

Once inside the church, evidence of its association with the family of the Marquis of Winchester and their home at Amport House, can be seen in the pulpit and in the low chancel screen rails, which were once the balusters of the staircase there. I was interested to learn also, from the very full historical account available in the church, that for over four hundred years the Manor of Quarley was in the hands of St. Katherine's Hospital in London, having been given to them by Henry VI in 1441. They leased out the Manor House, which once stood in the field to the south of the church, to various families, the last one of them being that of Richard Cox, the founder of Cox's Bank, paymasters to the army. The Cox family left Quarley Manor in 1821 and shortly afterwards it fell into disrepair, and was demolished. In the last century, as Cox's and King's [part of Lloyds], the bank was still paymaster or agent to the three services... I know this because I opened my first bank account at their branch in Pall Mall in 1957.

The Rector of Quarley throughout the whole period of the tenacy of Richard Cox, was Rev'd. Thomas Sheppard D.D. The wife he married in 1801 at the age of seventy-four [she being just thirty-one], was responsible for the building of the school in Amport in 1815; a year after his death.

ROMSEY ABBEY
St. Mary and St. Ethelfleda

In an age when not one man in a thousand could read, the church drove its lessons home in sculptured and vaulted space, and in the carvings and paintings of artists, who employed their genius to make the Christian story familiar to everyone.

Sir ARTHUR BRYANT   1899 - 1985

Whilst looking at the upper photograph opposite, you might like to imagine the strains of a hymn seeping through the early evening air, as the choir of Romsey Abbey conduct their rehearsal and the shadows imperceptibly lengthen across the greensward, where you or I may be sitting in the last, still warm, rays of a July sun. Before us rise the triple-storied ranks of Norman architecture "par-excellence", one almost wonders why they ever stopped building skywards in their enthusiasm to proclaim their religious credentials... probably it was the foundations. To us, the preposterous yet successful attempts to erect such buildings on ground very close to a river, as here and at Winchester and Salisbury, would have modern architects organising gangs with pile-drivers for months, before ever the first stone was laid. These buildings' wonderful survival teaches us a timely lesson... we may do it differently now, but do we do it better?

What we see before us today was not the original abbey, for King Edgar's patronage certainly had caused the foundations of an abbey to be laid in Romsey in 907, and it is likely that a religious community existed here some two hundred years earlier, as is known to be the case further down near the mouth of the River Test at Nursling. The Danes who destroyed the latter abbey may have destroyed the former too, yet it rose again in all its stone built magnificence between 1120 and 1180 and became the focus of a thriving town as well as a great religious institution, until the pestilence of The Black Death arrived in the late summer of 1348, and wiped out most of the occupants. Yet it revived, until the political threat of Henry VIII's 'Dissolution' [that caused many like abbeys to be destroyed or adapted to secular use], seemed about to overwhelm it once and for all. However, the townsfolk of Romsey had other ideas and subscribed £100 to buy it for their own parish church... to them, we and the world, owe a great debt of gratitude.

Within this abbey, the evidence of Sir Arthur Bryant's words is all around us; soaring vaults, carvings in stone and wood, effigies and monuments, and can there be any more wonderful example of late medieval painting than the reredos in the north transept, with its nine life-size saints and below, Christ himself rising from the tomb to the amazment of the Roman soldiers?

Of course examples of men's and women's artistic skills are still being added, to further enrich this Holy place. The brand new guide book is a "must" for any visitor, and there is always something new to learn... for example I did not know that St. Nicholas was both the patron saint of children and sailors; how right and proper therefore, that Earl Mountbatten's tomb should lie in the chapel dedicated to that saint in the south transept. I also noticed the carvings of what I took to be English Kings and Queens on the choir stalls. I cannot say I recognised them all, but Queen Victoria and Prince Albert were certainly there, on the front of one of the priests' stalls.

It is invidious to try to select any one aspect of this beautiful abbey, or any particular one of its treasures so lovingly protected within its walls as being the <u>most</u> remarkable. One's enduring memory of a visit to this place, may not be the architecture or the music or indeed the bells ringing out today over the town and meadows around, but simply the fact of its being there, massively reassuring as one century glides into another... after all it has seen so many. Perhaps, we may choose to summarise our experience, by recalling the words from that great hymn, which I remember we always sang on the last day of every term... perhaps some of you did too?.

O God our help in ages past,
Our hope for years to come,
Be thou our guard while troubles last,
And our eternal home.

ABBEY UNITED REFORMED CHURCH
ROMSEY

Be still and cool in thine own mind and spirit, from thine own thoughts,
and then thou wilt feel the principle of God...

GEORGE FOX 1624 - 1691

It was from such sentiments as these above or very similar ones, held by the two thousand or so dissenting pastors at the time of the Act of Uniformity [1662], that the Congregational and Presbyterian churches evolved. One such pastor was Rev'd. Thomas Warren of Houghton in Test Valley, who because of his principled opposition to the Act, even declined the offer of the post of Bishop of Salisbury, before the inevitable and consequential banishment from his "living".

Presumably he came to Romsey because he had other relations in the town, notably a certain John Warren, who had been installed as Vicar of Romsey during the period of The Commonwealth [1648-1662], and who also was ejected from his position, when he likewise refused to acknowledge the Book of Common Prayer etc. However, Rev'd. <u>Thomas</u> Warren was the founding father of this church, no doubt ably assisted by John and other family members. Of course it was an illegal, "underground" church to begin with, and had to meet secretly in peoples' homes, but eventually the political climate changed, and in 1672 their first meeting places could be officially licensed. Thomas Warren's cottage in Church Street, which was demolished in 1825, was one of four different premises so licensed for Non-conformist worship. Thomas Warren died in 1694, but not until 1888 when a wooden floor of the south transept of Romsey Abbey was lifted, was it discovered that he had been permitted burial within its walls, in spite of his Non-conformity.

The first proper Meeting House was built about 1708 on the opposite side of Abbey Water to that of the existing church. Nearly one hundred years passed before it needed replacement, and a new chapel on the present site was used for the first time in August 1804. It too, eventually had to be replaced in 1885, because it was too small for the congregation <u>and</u> the stream was undermining its foundations. Services were held in the Town Hall for the three years, during which time the present church was constructed. A separate Queen

Victoria's Jubilee Fund financed the impressive organ, with which it was equipped. The organ, though replaced by a new model in 1975, it is still a wonderful feature of the interior south wall and a fitting backdrop to the choir stalls and pulpit.

From the exterior, the church exhibits a "flowering" of Victorian Gothic style into Victorian Perpendicular, as the building rises up to its quite outstanding clerestory. Underneath the flint and bath stone architectural facing lies a core of solid brick. Inside everything "radiates" from the pulpit area; there is one central aisle and on either side two others fanning out into the pews, each of which must have been individually designed, since each has slightly different dimensions to cope with the angles. The nave however is rectangular, and formed by four arched arcades on the east and west sides, the arches being supported on square stone columns with inset Gothic designs. A fine gallery runs around three sides, and above, flooded with light from the nine huge clerestory windows, is a beautiful panelled ceiling in pale green and gold. This colour theme is repeated on the decorated organ pipes, of which I counted sixty-three, and also on the north wall, which is itself dominated by another immense perpendicular style window practically filling the whole wall-space. The glass in this window is in opaque Victorian pastel shades which tone with the interior decor extremely well. There are more conventional Gothic style windows at ground floor level, three of which are of stained glass; all are memorials. A double window under the north gallery commemorates those from this church who gave their lives in the two World Wars of the last century.

As I walked away towards the Newton Lane carpark, I glanced back at this edifice, this amalgam of styles, with its Italianate tower and its "tudor" wooden wall decoration on the side of the rooms above the road arch, and thought that someone had really decided to make a "statement" here. I think, they succeeded... I'm sure Thomas Warren would have been amazed.

ROMSEY BAPTIST CHURCH

Rich gifts of life and gladness, a new and heav'nly birth,
Baptismal waters flowing to cleanse the sons of earth;   ADA GREENAWAY. 1861 - 19??

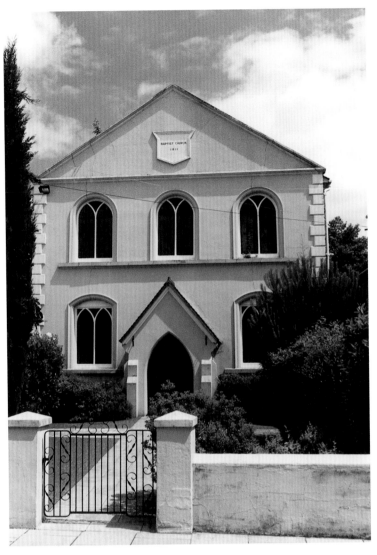

It is not known quite when the first Baptists met together in Romsey, but what is known, is that the first minister, the Rev'd. James Fanch was in post in 1750, and that a house in Middlebridge Street was first registered for preaching in 1751. This house was the centre for the Baptists until 1811 when the move was made to Bell Street.

The building stands back from the street frontage, and has a neat courtyard garden re-planted in 1991 with 'biblical plants and shrubs'; a sort of oasis in the midst of the bustle of Bell Street. The style of the front windows ressembles those of St. Deny's, Chilworth and St. Peter's Appleshaw; no doubt a fashion of the time. Inside, the hallway is separated by a stained glass screen from the main meeting room, and from it, there is access to the gallery. However, it is from the ground floor that the full impact of the gallery can be seen; a veritable masterpiece in artistic cast iron.

The present seating arrangements are apparently the result of a quite extensive re-design in 1992, which included the removal of the pews, in favour of chairs and a change in the orientation of the minister's desk, from the east end to the north side. The colour scheme is a tasteful shade of deep red, and nothing of the impact of the memorial stained glass windows of 1928 has been lost

in any way. All has not been a continuous upward trend for the Baptists of Romsey; it is recorded that the church survived the possibility of closure just before Christmas 1849, when numbers were low and debts were high... fifteen or so years later, numbers had reached over a hundred and all was well again.

At the time of the centenary, it was felt appropriate to install a new pipe organ and pulpit in celebration. Although electricity was installed in 1935, an electric blower for the organ had to wait until 1946. The organ was eventually replaced 'not without regret', by a modern electronic organ in the recent renovations of 1991-1992. It is a tribute to the Christian community in Romsey, that during this time, the Baptists' activities continued. I quote from the excellent booklet recalling this church's 250th anniversary... 'Our Sunday morning services were held in Romsey School; evening services and playgroup sessions were held in Romsey Abbey Church Rooms; Mens Contact Club in St. Joseph's Catholic Church; Womens Fellowship in the Methodist Church. A wedding was held in the United Reformed Church and Mums and Toddler's group met in the St. John's Ambulance Brigade H.Q.' Truly, a real Christian response to their needs by everyone... indeed, a beacon of hope, for a new century.

ROMSEY METHODIST CHURCH

The task Thy wisdom hath assign'd, O let me cheerfully fulfil;
In all my works Thy presence find, and prove Thy good and perfect Will.

CHARLES WESLEY 1707 - 1788

I'm quite sure Charles Wesley, whose speciality was hymn writing, would be pleased and honoured that over two hundred years after his death, his hymns are still held in high regard. Although he and his famous brother John did not always see "eye to eye", their partnership was the bedrock of Methodism, and provided a wonderful transfusion of faith into a society that was losing touch with its roots. This was the time when agricultural land was being enclosed by the wealthy, and people were forced, or drawn, into the centres of the industrial revolution. In these places the established churches were either apathetic to, or overwhelmed by, the task suddenly before them... that of proclaiming the good news of the Gospel to an urban multitude.

It was not just in the industrial centres that Methodism took root, and the Methodists of Romsey became a significant group. It is well to remember that John Wesley's avowed aim was to rejuvenate the <u>Church of England</u>, not to create schism; the final break only occurred after his death.

An example of the first signs of separation, may be found hanging on the wall in this church. A legal document dated 19th January 1800, drawn up by the Registrar of the Diocese of Winchester on the orders of the Lord Bishop, licensing the house of Moses Comley

for Non-conformist worship. I presume this must have been the first autonomous Wesleyan Methodist Congregation in the town. By 1813 the first Wesleyan Chapel was built in Banning Street and must have been of some size, being referred to in 1874 as being able to hold 386 persons. Its size would account for the not inconsiderable cost of £1,500, all of which was "put up" by one man, Mr. P. Jewell. Regrettably, this benefactor died suddenly and had left no documentation supporting his intended gift to the Society, and the trustees therefore were faced with an enormous debt when Mr. Jewell's executors demanded the money be refunded. Suffice it to say that all these complications eventually had a satisfactory outcome.

By 1875 the Banning St. Chapel was considered to be 'in a street notorious for wickedness', so the site in The Hundred was bought and the former chapel became the Citadel of The Salvation Army, [as also happened in Andover]. The new church opened its doors on 31st May 1882. New extensions were built in 1982 to celebrate the centenary and more recently the whole interior has been redesigned and refurbished. The colour scheme, 'of lavender shades', has picked out the tones of the stained glass in the windows and created a very peaceful and tasteful environment for worship.

ROMSEY ROMAN CATHOLIC CHURCH
St. Joseph

For my thoughts are not your thoughts
neither are your ways my ways, saith the Lord.
For as the heavens are higher than the earth,
so are my ways higher than your ways
and my thoughts than your thoughts....
... so shall my word be that goeth forth out of my mouth:
it shall not return to me void,
but it shall accomplish that which I please....

Book of the Prophet ISAIAH. Chap 55

On February 17th 1912 a doctor warned a mother in London, that her daughter's death might occur at any moment. The daughter was twenty-two years old and had been ill for nearly ten years, and for the previous fortnight had been unconscious and blind, fed only by injection. On the very next day in the <u>presence</u> of her family and friends, she was miraculously made <u>completely well</u>, she suddenly sat up in bed and asked for food,... her name was Dorothy Kerin. After the notoriety surrounding her case she came to live in Thruxton. She founded "Burswood" near Tunbridge Wells and lived to the age of 72.

On April 7th 1927, a doctor warned the sisters of the convent in Romsey, that the death of one of their number might occur at any moment. His patient was 28 years old and had been ill for nearly five years, and could no longer eat or drink and had lost the use of her legs. On the 8th April during a two minute absence from her bedside by the Mother Provincial, she was miraculously made <u>completely well</u>; she suddenly got out of bed, announced her cure to her amazed friends, and next morning had bacon and egg for breakfast. Her name was Sister Gerard and she subsequently spent 40 years as a missionary in Africa, living to the age of 87.

For us, these two so similar yet unconnected events, show quite conclusively the wisdom of the Biblical words quoted above; perhaps we should ponder them more often than we do. True wholeness and healing are matters not only of mind and body but equally of the spirit. We are apt to think we know it all... we don't, and never will.

Sister Gerard's room in the Convent of the La Sagesse Sisters, is maintained today more or less as it was on the occasion of the miracle. The adjoining chapel of the convent subsequently became the parish church of the Roman Catholic Parish of Romsey in about 1961, and was dedicated to St. Joseph. So much of the modern history of Catholicism in Romsey is linked to the sisters of the La Sagesse Convent, that it is impossible to comment on the one without the other. 'The Daughters of Wisdom' had been founded by Louis de Montfort in Brittany in 1703, to care for the sick and to educate the young. At the same time, he founded the company of priests that became the Montfort Missionaries. Nearly two hundred years later [in 1891] the bishop of the new Catholic Diocese of Portsmouth, invited some of the sisters to come to England, to set up a home in Alton for the mentally ill, but they were not well received there. Almost immediately they moved to Romsey to set up an orphanage instead. Ten years later the French Government passed a law to have 'Religious Congregations' banned in France, and so the Montfort Missionaries had to find another home, eventually they too came to Romsey, and established their Montfort College a mile from the town.

St. Joseph's was built in its present form in 1913, and is an impressive example of the art of ornamental bricklaying. In the driveway stands a statue of St. Louis de Montfort, who was canonised in 1947 largely as a result of Sister Gerard's testimony. Inside, apart from the tilework around the arches of the windows and the gilded Stations of The Cross, the walls are pristine white... the roof is similarly decorated. There is a south gallery or organ loft supported by an enormous timber beam across the entire width of the nave; there are no side aisles. Marble steps lead up into the sanctuary and the altar is supported on short marble columns, on either side are chapels. Behind this is a stone reredos backlit by a semicircular window, on which can be seen the dove of the Holy Spirit descending. All the windows are of opaque glass, slightly tinted, their chief joy being in their wonderfully intricate leading. We found it an attractive and Holy place.

ROWNHAMS
St. John the Evangelist

He that sat on the throne said, 'Behold I make all things new... It is done. I am Alpha and Omega, the beginning and the end. I will give unto him that is athirst of the fountain of the water of life, freely.'　　Revelation of St. JOHN　Chapter 21

St. John's was built on "derelict land" given by the Chamberlayne family. It was begun by Major William Colt, completed by his widow, and first consecrated on 25th October 1855. The architect was Rev'd. William Grey [a descendant of the family of Lady Jane Grey, Queen of England for nine days in 1553]. He had a strong link with two other Test Valley parishes, having married Harriet White in Abbotts Ann church in 1849, and she was a grand-daughter of Rev'd. Henry White of Fyfield. It is a fine building faced in light grey Plymouth Winstone, with distinctive features, such as the windows and the lattice belltower openings, in honey-coloured Caen stone. This church, and the other St. John's at Lockerley, are the only two with stone-clad spires in the whole borough.

There is an interesting architectural variety to the tracery in the windows, [I only saw two matching pairs] but it is what they contain, which is unique in Test Valley, namely fifty-four examples of Flemish glass medallions of the 16th and 17th centuries, sympathetically set within matching gold opaque Victorian designs; a most amazing collection. Thankfully, they were not damaged during the last war, as the east and west windows were. The west window once held stained glass of the four apostles... only one survived the

blast... appropriately St. John!

St. John's also has historical links with Ampfield, for it was to this church that Rev'd. R. F. Wilson, came in 1860. It was he who started the magazine in 1865, which to this day continues to provide a wonderful record of the parish. The peal of tubular bells was added in 1889 in his memory.

On the day of my visit, not only the altar, but every windowsill and ledge was decorated with flowers of white and deep red, so many that it seemed a wedding was anticipated. I made an enquiry but found that I was wrong, such standards are customary here.

The font is at the west end, and has a counter-balanced top in the design of a Gothic spire, complete with lucarnes and crockets. Doubling as a south transept, is the ground floor of the tower [since 1967 a Lady Chapel], and still with the original entrance door. The chancel floor has been extended into the width of the nave, to provide a small carpeted stage area, and I noticed both the pulpit of 1906, and the lectern are 'fully wired for sound'. The sanctuary has an interesting Italian marble and alabaster reredos, which was presented in 1872. In spite of its 19th century origins, this church had lively modern feel, with conspicuous wall-space devoted to the activities of its most junior members.

SHERFIELD ENGLISH
St. Leonard

And into that gate shall they enter, and in that house shall they dwell, where there shall be no Cloud nor Sun, no darkness nor dazzling, but one equal light...

JOHN DONNE 1572 - 1631

This church was born out of an expression of a mother's grief... that of Louisa Caroline, Lady Ashburton, for her daughter Mary, Marchioness of Northampton, who died at the age of forty-one in 1902. Sadly it became her own memorial for she died also the following year. The great west window shows them united once more, in its lower righthand panel, where Lady Ashburton is shown holding out to Jesus and the attendant archangels the church itself as an offering. Beneath, an enormous brass plaque is fulsome in its praise for her. There is a picture of her on the windowsill in the south-west corner, at the local school, which was an earlier benefaction, in 1871.

The building seems to typify the power and influence of the British Empire in its heyday; the houses of the rich were like cathedrals, the churches they built, like great country houses. There is an elegance in the florishes of a new architectural style; gone are the needle-pointed spires and lancets, gone are the flounces of Victorian Decorated... heralding the new century is an Edwardian version of Perpendicular. Obviously no expense was spared in creating this "fourth edition" of St. Leonard's, as all traces of the past were swept away in a feast of mellow brick and stone, culminating in the octagon tower with its distinctive flying buttresses. I'm sure Hugo

D'Engley [1304] Lord of the Manor of Sherfield, [and first known rector] would be impressed.

The country house atmosphere is enhanced by tended borders of roses, forget-me-nots, primulas etc., and inside it is exemplified by the plethora of prints, plaques, watercolours and photographs that abound on its walls. In the south aisle, the memorial to the fallen of the Great War is unique in Test Valley, for having photographs of each of the ten men in service dress. Nearby is a more usual brass plaque and beneath it a simple poppy wreath. The stained glass east window is a slightly smaller version of the west window in design, and depicts in its upper sections a crucifixion scene, and in the lower, a scene of the nativity entitled, 'And the Word was made flesh and dwelt among us'. All other windows in the church are ornamented in their upper tracery only, with leaded shapes of fruit or flowers in muted colours.

The nave itself is of four bays, and the columns and arches match that of the chancel arch, beside which stands a wonderful Jacobean pulpit faced with panel carvings of Temperance, Justice and Love. A fine screen, upon the top of which is carved 'The grace of our Lord Jesus Christ be with you all', divides the chancel from the nave... a real blessing to carry with you on your departure.

SHIPTON BELLINGER
St. Peter

Breathes there the man, with soul so dead, who never to himself hath said,
This my own my native land! Whose heart hath ne'er within him burned, as home his
footsteps he hath turned, from wandering on a foreign strand!

The Lay of the Last Ministrel.   Sir WALTER SCOTT 1771 - 1832

The comings and goings to and from a *foreign strand* are familiar to this village, positioned right on the edge of the Army's Salisbury Plain Training Area. In the fields around here the volunteers of this country and the Commonwealth were encamped, before going to the front in the First World War, and this was repeated in 1940-1945. Sir Walter Scott's words above ring true for all, who returning from abroad find repose and contentment in the countryside of England. We are reminded of the well-known words of a famous song by the American, J.H.Payne... 'Be it ever so humble, there's no place like home'. Perhaps also the ancestors of W.S.Gilbert, who are buried here, would likewise agree, using his words from The Gondoliers... 'Of that there is no manner of doubt; no probable, possible shadow of doubt, no possible doubt whatever!'

The booklet produced in 1986 called 'The story of our village', informs us that the word Shipton is most likely a derivation of the Anglo-Saxon "Sceap Tun" meaning sheep farm, and the word "Bellinger" refers to Ingram Berenger, who became Lord of the Manor in 1297... he was probably the builder of the first church.

Once again externally, the church has a familiar 'medieval village' appearance. Its setting could hardly be more delightful, since it is sited well back from, and above

the level of the River Bourne, and has to be reached by a footbridge from the village street. This is especially necessary in the spring, with the river in full flow. Beneath the lovely beech tree on the north side of the church stands a garden bench, a Millennium gift from the village fete... appreciated by many we expect.

Inside, although there is only one window on the south side of the nave and two on the north, sufficient light pours in through a large west window. It depicts three scenes from the life of St. Peter entitled, 'Follow me'; 'Arise Quickly', and 'Feed my Sheep', which we take to be Peter's 'calling', his release by the angel from prison, and his commission to proclaim the Word. The window itself is a memorial to a lady named Frances Fowle, who died in 1865.

At the entrance to the chancel, beneath the pointed arch is an unusual stone screen of Victorian Gothic style, having three "bays" of a three-cusped design. This same theme is repeated in carved wood on the front of the altar, [with the actual frontal cloth hanging behind], and again on the reredos, where the stonework background is painted with lilies.

One has the feeling that this parish is a "happy posting" for its incumbents... the evidence for this is visible in the east window, if you care to look.

SMANNELL
Christ Church

Sorrow with his pick mines the heart, but he is a cunning workman... he deepens the channels whereby happiness may enter, and he hollows out new chambers for joy to abide in, when he is gone.   Author unknown.

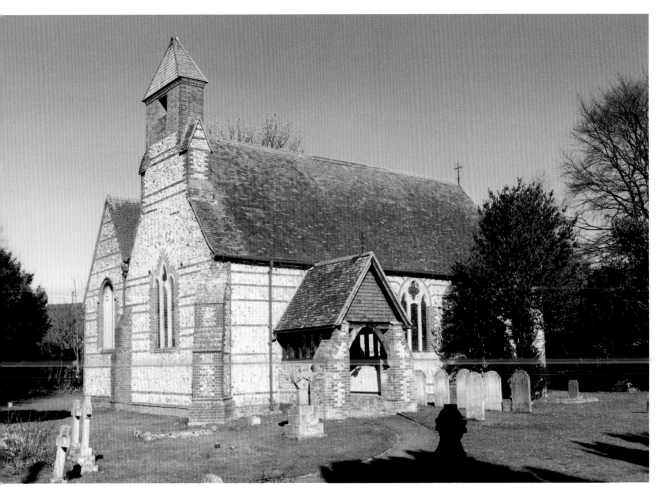

Smannell Church, just a couple of miles north-east of Andover was built in 1857; its architect was William White, who also built Christ Church, Hatherden in the same year. He was the great-nephew of Gilbert White of Selborne. Although the two churches are not twins, both are faced in flint with horizontal lines of brick, and the brick detailing around the windows is exactly the same. Each has four apse windows, and each one has a "dominant" window in the south wall of the nave. The internal walls of this church are brick with a subtle use of different colours, and the chancel is painted above the pannelling with a trellis and floral design, in accordance with the architect's original plans.

The words of the verse above seemed to us to have been written with the theme of the west window in mind. This large stained glass window, depicts the scene described in St. Luke, chapter 7, where Jesus restores to life the only son of a widow of the city of Nain. A marble plaque tells us that this window was given by a widow, Mrs. Earle, in memory of her son, Lt. John Earle, who was killed in action in West Africa in June 1915. This lovely window, is a poignant reminder for all those who have felt the *pick that mines the heart*, under similar tragic circumstances.

The Earle family of Enham Place were great benefactors of this church. The three 'I am' stained glass windows in the apse, 'I am the bread of life; 'I am the good shepherd', and 'I am the true vine' are in memory of Lt. Col. W. H. Earle. In 1894, Mrs Earle financed the construction of the north aisle and the choir vestry and also gave the organ. The only window in the south wall of the nave is another Earle memorial of 1891. When we saw it, it was a triumphant explosion of colour with the sun fiercely illuminating the figures of St.Paul, and his chief companions on his first and second missionary journeys, St. Barnabas, and St. Silas.

In the north aisle there is an excellent Millennium window by Lilian Shaw of Norfolk. This window's centre-piece, is a timeless depiction of a mother holding up her son to the heavens, with the dove of the Holy Spirit descending. 'Timeless', because the barefoot mother and her baby are carefully not dressed in any way in which their 'time' can be identified. This contrasts with the treatment of the side panels, where clearly the old is on the left, and the present day on the right.

Before our departure, we thought how fitting it was, that the excellent light oak pews commissioned from the workshops for disabled ex-servicemen in Enham, should have been made on the same property as was once owned by the munificent Earle family.

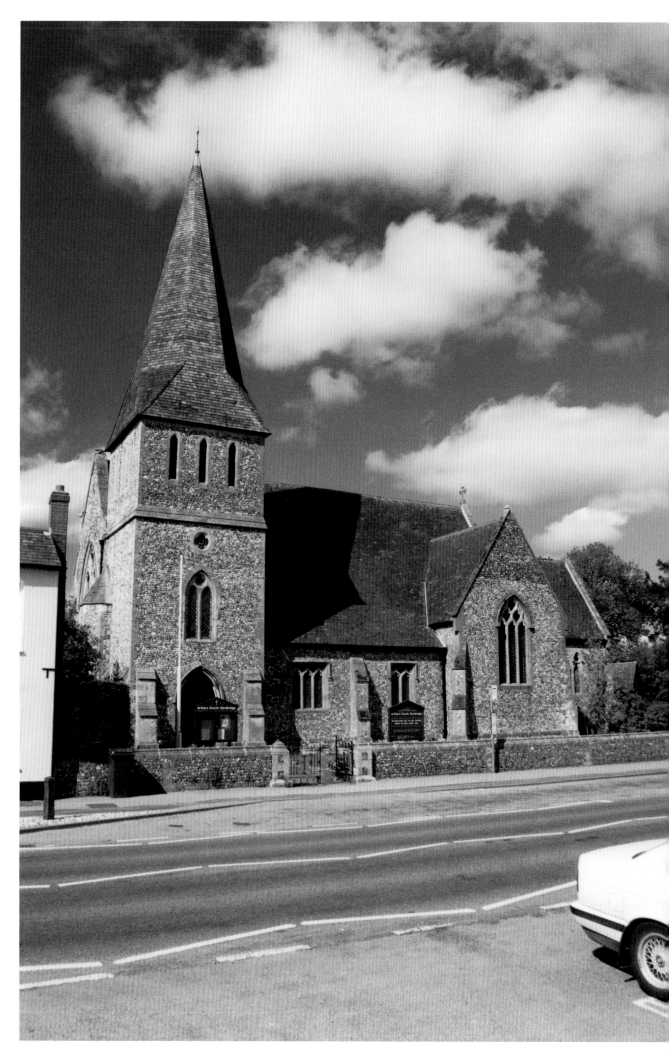

STOCKBRIDGE
St. Peter

Let the blessing of St. Peter's Master be... upon all
that are lovers of virtue, and dare trust in His providence...
...be quiet, and go a-angling.

The Compleat Angler
IZAAK WALTON 1593 - 1683.

I confess to knowing little or nothing about angling, but it seems to me a happy coincidence to have found the above quotation for this piece, I hope that those more expert in such matters, such as the members of the exclusive Houghton Club, will think likewise.

With new signs recently erected at the time of writing, heralding Stockbridge as the 'Heart of The Test Valley', [an apt description], this popular small town will surely add to its reputation as a most pleasant place to visit. The spacious main street already draws crowds of ramblers, shoppers and visitors throughout the year to where once, only the stage coaches and drovers with their flocks were likely to stop. In the heart of the main street stands "new" St. Peter's Church, always open, built in 1866 by John Colson of Winchester, [St.John's, Lockerley was another of his churches]. I was surprised to discover that Stockbridge only became a parish in its own right in 1842, having previously been one of the dependent chapels under the Parish of Kings Somborne for probably at least 1000 years. Old St. Peter's still exists at the eastern end of the town, but only the chancel remains, though in good repair and still used for sevices. As much as possible of the building materials of that church were re-used in the construction of the new one. It was the imminent arrival of the railway that accounted for the church's move to its present position, sadly that link with Southampton has long since gone.

From its Victorian beginnings St. Peter's has certainly moved with the times, as any casual visitor will see immediately on entering. Within the porch, one's eye and interest is captured at once by a war memorial plaque, and on the window sill above, I found a display of poppies and poppy wreaths. Once inside it is likely you will hear a gentle background music of familiar pieces, and be drawn to glance at the display of second-hand books for sale, discretely tucked away at the rear of the south aisle. Almost all of the western end of the nave has been converted to a reception area, with its own facilities for casual refreshment after services, and no doubt at other times too I suspect, for those who provide the excellent floral displays.

The Lady Chapel, which occupies the space of the south transept, holds one of the "gems" in the possession of St. Peter's, in the form of a renovated but, in its centre, a very old depiction of the crucifixion in stone, barely twelve inches high I should think. To me it looked as though it could easily be of Saxon workmanship, but the guide book seems to think it is later. Apparently the fact that Christ's feet are shown nailed separately [as on the 9th century rood in Romsey Abbey] is indeed a Saxon tradition inherited from the Eastern Orthodox Church. Interestingly, the crucifixion scene in the stained-glass east window of neighbouring Longstock Church, [made in Munich in 1882], has the same positioning for the feet of Christ. As one might expect to see in a church of this vintage, the wall behind the main altar is richly decorated.

Examples of needle-craft abound in this church; not least the attractive patchwork cover of the nave altar with all the stitched crosses on it, and the seventy or more kneelers with the usual variety of subjects. I saw one with a list of names of 'Christian Heros' from St. Peter to Billy Graham, including King Alfred, Erasmus and Wesley, all in historical order. Another with the badges of Chester and Amsterdam, one with a picture of Taskers No. 4 Plough, and yet another quoting Proverbs 31, verse 13 'She seeks wool and flax and works willingly with her hands'. A fitting collective commentary and tribute, I thought, to all who had laboured to produce such examples of skill and artistry. High in the mostly clear glass west window is the newly installed stained-glass badge of Stockbridge, and underneath the Roman numerals M.M.

Stockbridge as a crossing point of the River Test has always been of strategic importance. There is evidence of the defensive ramparts of ancient forts high on either side of the valley, which now belie the peaceful scene below. This, centred on St. Peter's is thankfully free of the threat of conflict as once was often the case, and may it remain so forever.

TANGLEY
St. Thomas of Canterbury

*If a man will begin with certainties, he shall end in doubts; but if he will be content
to begin with doubts, he shall end in certainties.*

FRANCIS BACON 1561 - 1626

We first discovered this little church in 1968 whilst walking with our children from near The Fox Inn, up through the bluebell woods... suddenly it appeared! We did not go in on that occasion, and in fact it was not until after retirement in 1994, having set ourselves the task to photograph all the Test Valley churches, that I arrived at the gate to St.Thomas', camera in hand, and sought the key. It turned out to be quite inspirational.

The site of St. Thomas' is thought to have been of a religious nature for longer than anyone can tell. The church history relates its rebuilding in 1875, and comments that the apse was reconstructed on pre-existing foundations; were they Saxon I wonder? Being only "yards" from the Roman Road from Winchester to Cirencester, perhaps there could have been a wayside Roman temple on this site? The three sarsen stones in the churchyard; could they be a clue to even earlier religious significance? Perhaps, who knows?

However, it would be quite wrong to ignore its present day charms, for here is a church of great interest in a beautiful setting. The pathway leads up on the south side, past the little apse almost hidden behind a magnolia bush. Inside, almost blocking your progress, is Hampshire's only font made entirely of lead, it is a fine tub-shaped object with five relief designs, one is of three fleur-de-lis

and the others are of a tudor rose and a crown above a thistle, [both duplicated]... we are told that it belongs to the early 17th century. At this end of the church a Gothic arch springing from carved corbels forms the entrance to the carpeted ringing chamber of the tower, wherein hang six bells. Notices on the walls record special bell-ringing events, one involving 5,040 changes. The same claret-coloured carpet softens your footsteps as you walk down the centre of the small nave; I hope for you there will still be flowers on every windowsill. A small step differentiates the nave from the choir and there is a similar one at the altar rail. Above, a Gothic arch of the original church, forms the entrance into the apse, where stands the altar. The sanctity of this minute holy recess [photograph on page 7] cannot be explained in words... the light falling through the little side-windows never fails to lend an aura to the simple setting.

If a man will begin... with doubts, he shall end with certainties. Surely most of us start with doubts and pray that we may be given time to find the certainties. I suspect that they are all around us, if we care to look? As a child, I did not doubt that the world was round; but it was when I saw the curving horizon from high altitude as a Canberra bomber pilot, that the sight awakened an awareness of the immensity of the universe.

THRUXTON
St. Peter and St. Paul

*So when primroses pave the way, and the sun warms the stone, we may
receive the exile spirit coming into its own.*   C. DAY. LEWIS   1904 - 1972

You have only to walk through the smart wrought-iron gates with their little green-painted leaves and up the path a little way, to see spread out before you under an amazing weeping beech tree the scene above [taken in March 1998], where the primroses year after year respond to the warming influence of the slowly lengthening days. I've no doubt they were here long before the first church was built... even the present one dates from 1240, though very much repaired and rebuilt between 1850 and 1877. What it may lack in architectural purity it more than makes up for in individuality; the photograph shows there is a very elaborate priest's doorway, and what seems to be the top of a previous window re-used at a much lower level!

Into the porch, is also straight into the base of the tower and ringing chamber, before one passes through a pair of modern draught-proof glass doors into the really quite tiny nave. It doesn't feel small because the north aisle gives added width and there in all its glory is the refurbished font, and cover newly finished in goldleaf, scarlet and dark blue... the result of a parish Millennium project. This is only the first of many treasures that this church holds... look up and you will see 'improving texts' of the Victorian era on almost every surface. In the chancel aisle, and kindly revealed to me by the

churchwarden, was the carpet-covered eight and a half foot memorial brass of Sir John Lisle [inset in the stone floor] dated 1407. It is the earliest known example in the <u>whole country</u>, of a knight wearing full plate armour.

There are no transepts on this church, but there are the remains of two 16th century Chantry Chapels, inside which are the carved stone effigies of their donors, worthy of any cathedral. Here also was something rather unusual in my experience, an unpainted wooden effigy of a lady dressed in Elizabethan costume... Lady Elizabeth Philpott, who died in 1616. The fine carving of her ruff and dress had withstood the passage of time very well, but sadly not her facial features. Her diminutive size, I thought, was probably accurate.

The excellent Church History available to visitors records that the east window and the vestry stained glass windows are the work of Thomas Willement, who was 'stained glass artist to Queen Victoria'.

As I walked back down the path towards the former rectory, I recalled that it was to this village that Dr. Langford-James came as Rector in 1919, bringing with him Dorothy Kerin, whose miraculous healing in 1912 had become of international interest. The circumstances of her recovery, were so similar to that experienced by Sister Gerard in Romsey in 1927.

TIMSBURY
St. Andrew

In country churches old and pale I hear the changes smoothly rung, and watch the coloured sallies fly from rugged hands to rafters high, as round and back the bells are swung.

Church of England Thoughts
Sir JOHN BETJEMAN 1906 - 1984

Here we have one such *old and pale* country church... on this average summer's day the changing light from a slightly clouded sky washes over its walls, creating alternately tones of grey and ochre, just like a Cotswold wall recently repaired with newly quarried stone. The shadows cast by the silver grey oak of the porch on the south side, lean in a protective way over the almost tottering headstones nearby, and... but we are getting ahead of ourselves!

The approach to the church, signposted from the A 3057 Romsey main road, is much improved since I first visited in 1994, and on arrival the scene before you, will be the one in the photograph. On the exterior of the south walls of both chancel and nave you will no doubt notice three memorial plaques, unfortunately I could not read them. Apart from the little dormer window in the roof beyond the porch, there is only one window in the nave on this side, but do not for one moment imagine this affects the enjoyment of the interior, for which any journey, from any distance, is worth all the "effort".

I've no doubt that Betjeman had in mind a greater number of bellringers, tolling a greater number of bells than there are at St. Andrew's, when he wrote the words above. Here there are only three, but nowhere will they have been more carefully and regularly rung. What brings

me to this conclusion, is the new Millennium window in the west wall beneath the bell tower, where an old doorway once was. It is dedicated to Bill Watkinson a ringer here for over 40 years. This quite beautiful window shows him both at work and in recreation, the brickmaker and the angler. Above the startling colours of kingfishers on one side, and the more sombre brick kilns on the other, are words which he would have understood so well, 'Unless the Lord build the house, its builder labours in vain'.

It is understandable that on entry, the eyes should fall firstly on the window just described above, but stop and look about you... to the left of the doorway on the floor is a fine oak 13th century parish chest [the oldest in Test Valley I believe] and on the wall above is a unique 'library cupboard', on which is carved the name of the donor and the date 1713.

Further down the church, you will see that the light from the solitary nave window on the south wall falls invitingly upon a glass-topped desk cabinet; look inside and there is a chained Bible of 1613 opened to an appropriate page of scripture. On the other side is the very splendid oak pulpit; above it the words, 'Wo is unto me if I preach not the Gospel'. Between them is a quite rare chancel screen of the early 15th century.

UPPER CLATFORD
All Saints

Summer's pleasures they are gone like to visions every one, and the cloudy
days of autumn and of winter cometh on. I tried to call them back but unbidden they
are gone...   JOHN CLARE 1793 - 1864

To find All Saints Church from the village street, you still have to go up and over the bridge, under which the barges, and later the trains, from Southampton used to wind the last mile or so to the centre of Andover. In fact this church lies in respectable and splendid isolation amid the water-meadows, in a most peaceful setting. Just a few yards beyond the churchyard flows the River Anton. In the photograph the mists of a November morning filter through the pollarded limes and between the gravestones, leaving watery droplets in their wake. We may imagine grass and trees alike, awaiting the promise of the sun to absorb the valley mist, and throw slanting beams of warmth into the picture, thus once again visually re-uniting church and village.

One enters through a lychgate dated 1905, beside which is the War Memorial cross and a smart flagstaff. The pathway leads straight to the brick porch and main door, and is flanked by an avenue of yews, variegated hollies and the limes already mentioned. Inside the church is a small brass plaque, which records the lychgate being given in memory of a parishioner, ' by his friends and neighbours'. The door itself is worth a second glance for over the years it has accumulated its fair share of graffiti. I noticed for example the date 1699 alongside some initials, and a "secret" peephole through

its planks.

All Saints has an unusually wide nave and the only double chancel arch I have ever seen. The Victoria County History explains that this is the result of alterations done in the 17th century when the original north aisle was incorporated into the nave. The new nave required a widened chancel, and so, because the span was too great for a single arch, some columns and two arches of the old Norman north arcade were reconstructed across the gap! In the nave itself the roof beams are supported centrally by wooden posts.

On the south wall of the nave are some First World War memorials to the sons of the Allen family. I noticed one recorded the death of 'The last surviving son...' the poignancy of the parents' experience of their losses, can be read quite clearly on the inscriptions.

A 17th century pulpit with an octagonal tester stands at one side of the chancel entrance and within it, what may be a small misericord seat. The whole of the nave, north aisle, and the sanctuary, are oak panelled; the former in commemoration of the Silver Jubilee of George V in 1935. Standing in the sanctuary is an unusual 14th century pillar piscina, rediscovered by the rector inside the tower in 1909. The tower itself has a plaque within it giving its construction date as 1578.

UPPER ELDON
St. John the Baptist

The unwearied sun from day to day does his Creator's power display, and publishes,
to every land the works of an Almighty Hand.

JOSEPH ADDISON   1672 - 1719

This is one of those places where you have to almost pinch yourself to be convinced that you have arrived. Upper Eldon Church is situated high on the eastern side of the Test Valley, some two miles south of Kings Somborne. Having driven along a road, which is often so narrow as to make you hope that you are the only traveller, you arrive at a smart drive to a farmhouse. A well-tended lawn, a child's swing and a football repose centre stage, and moreover, there on the left, also in the front garden... the church itself!

Up here, *the works of an Almighty Hand* are much in evidence. The freshness of the air, the brightness of the clouds, and in the spring not only the scent and sight of the bluebell woods en route, but that of the beautiful white lilac standing beside the front door of the church... all these contribute to the sense of occasion.

Push back the door and a cool austerity lingers all around you, the daylight is reflected from the unadorned white walls, and you are aware of a beautiful simplicity, in which a chair, a tiny desk and a little wooden altar become as artistic as a masterpiece by Vermeer. The very absence of ornament creates a stage, a tableau, in which you are an integral part; your every movement, the very act of breathing becomes significant; the result of a heightened consciousness, as if an unseen audience were there to

focus their attention upon you.

The history of Upper Eldon is full of references to dilapidations, though happily it retains most of its original lancet windows. It seems that in every century someone has had to restore this building, in some form or other... the whole of the east wall fell down and was rebuilt in 1729, and the church lost two feet of its miniscule length in the process. Some consecration crosses, of which there were once nine, have been lost; now only their stone moulded bases remain to tantalise us as to how they looked.

Upper Eldon <u>has</u> figured in history to a limited extent; first it was given to the New Minster in Winchester in 1043 by Queen Emma, [wife of both Ethelred and Canute], in gratitude for her acquital, after her trial in Winchester Cathedral. Later it figured in the endowments given to Mottisfont Priory in 1201 by its founder William Briwere, Sheriff of Hampshire. The priory was designed to house about twelve Augustinian Canons, or 'Austin Friars'. At the Dissolution of the Monasteries in 1536, Mottisfont was given by Henry VIII to his Lord Chamberlain, Lord William Sandys, in exchange for the villages of Chelsea and Paddington... I suppose it looked a good enough deal at the time, or perhaps it was not a good idea to argue with the king!

114

VALLEY PARK
St. Francis

Merciful God... Grant that we may not seek so much to be consoled, as to console;
To be understood, as to understand, to be loved, as to love.

Prayer of St. FRANCIS of ASSISI 1181 - 1226

Were we to have been at Dover at the right time in 1224, we would have seen a group of nine religious brethren ['freres' in French; 'friars' in English], disembarking after a Channel crossing. Three of them were English and they were the first followers of St. Francis to arrive in this country. Their founder was the son of a wealthy clothier living in what today we call Northern Italy. After a year spent as a prisoner of war, Francis returned to the comforts of home, but in 1206 he renounced a life of ease and decided to become a hermit. On 24th February 1209, he heard, in church, the story from the 10th chapter of St. Matthew's Gospel, of the sending out of the disiples by Jesus to preach to the poor and the lepers, and he felt called to do the same sort of ministry. With the Pope's approval he and his first followers set forth, barefoot and dressed only in cloaks of grey material gathered at the waist with rope, [the Greyfriars], begging their way from place to place, preaching to the poor and destitute, and healing the sick... as far as they were able.

St. Francis believed in the "all-inclusiveness" of God's creation here on Earth, so he also ventured to the Holy Land to try to convert the Muslims... but without success. The inclusiveness was reflected in his desire that Franciscans could come from any background, provided that they proclaimed the Catholic faith and acccepted the principles of poverty and chastity.

It is interesting to note that this church in Valley Park, demonstrates a modern concept of inclusiveness in that here, in the one building, exists a Christian Community of three different denominations, Church of England, Methodist and United Reformed. The embryo parish came into existence, very appropriately on the eve of Trinity Sunday 1987; already plans were in hand to create the church and the adjacent school. The architect was James Lunn-Rockliffe RIBA. As work commenced, an oak casket made by Philip Watts, a parishioner, and containing soil from Assisi and from Valley Park was placed in the foundations of the sanctuary on 6th September 1990. The church was completed in July 1991, and dedicated by the Bishop of Winchester on 4th October 1991. Coincident with this event came the legal formation of the Anglican Parish and formal establishment of the Ecumenical Partnership.

The photograph shows the church from the south-east with the glass south wall of the nave opening directly onto the patio and lawn area. Just visible on the left of the picture, is The Garden of Remembrance, in which stands a large copper cross, once a feature on the tower of the church in Bernard Street, Southampton.

VERNHAM DEAN
St. Mary the Virgin

For the beauty of the earth, for the beauty of the skies, for the love which from our birth, over and around us lies; Lord of all to Thee we raise, this our grateful hymn of praise.

F. S. PIERPOINT 1835 - 1917

Had this church not needed to be rebuilt in 1851, it would have been yet one more example of the medieval village style; that is to say, there would have been a nave and chancel as they are today, plus a south porch and a small shingled bell turret at the western end. It is likely that there have been three previous churches on this site from the 11th century onwards; the Norman stonework of the west doorway is a relic of one such.

In Vernham Dean, as in Test Valley in general, *the beauty of the earth*, and equally *the beauty of the skies* as the accompanying photograph shows, is obvious. Knowing that music in this church is highly regarded, we trust that our quotation above will be acceptable.

The heavy buttressing of all the walls may be a clue as to why the previous rebuilds were necessary, for St. Mary's is on a relatively small platform on a steeply sloping site. The scaffolding inside was evidence of recent remedial action, necessary following the discovery of serious cracks in 1995. However, we found there was much to admire, not least the attractive three-branch candelabra on every alternate pew. At roof level one's attention is also immediately drawn to the six almost life-size trumpeting angels in silhouette, clad in blue with almost real, wreaths of roses on their heads.

The windows have a basic stone framework similar, though less elaborate, to those of Monxton [1854] and Wherwell [1856], paired in the nave and single in the chancel. The nave windows are clear diamond-paned glass except for the easternmost pair, which have opaque gold patterns. The chancel windows are all of biblical scenes, some being memorials to local people. The east window is a pleasing group of five lancets, thought to have been designed by a former incumbent and may have been made in Germany. A Victorian octagonal font is situated midway in the nave on the north side, surrounded on three sides with inward facing pews. In the floor of the nave aisle there are several 18th century stone grave slabs. High above on the tall chancel arch hangs a Hanoverian Royal Coat of Arms, dated 1838, with the letters VIC I REG beside it.

On the oak lectern is a well-polished brass plaque recording its dedication to a former 'Priest of this Parish 1886-1906' [Revd. F. J. Leeper], and is inscribed also with the words 'Thy Word is a Lantern unto my Feet and a Light unto my Path'. On the nave wall adjacent, is a fine wooden War Memorial.

St Mary's was only established as a separate parish in 1871, then in 1901 it was joined with Linkenholt. In 1979 it returned with Linkenholt to its original "parent parish" of Hurstbourne Tarrant.

WEST TYTHERLEY
St. Peter

*Where we may trace each streamlet through the meadow, where we can
follow every fitful shadow, where we can watch the winds among the corn, and see
the waves along the forest borne.*
Author unknown

Both the Tytherley churches are dedicated to St. Peter. Approaching from the neighbouring village of East Tytherley, this one stands high on a bank overlooking the site of an older church, where the road to Frenchmoor goes off to the left. Having entered the churchyard, pause for a moment to look back upon the open valley along which you have just come, set out like a landscape by Constable. Quite literally a place where in spring most certainly *we may trace each streamlet through the meadow,... and see the waves along the forest borne.*

In the Domesday Book the church is noted as a chapelry of the church at Mottisfont, as indeed were many others around here. Looking at the photograph it can be seen that it was rebuilt in two stages; a plaque on the wall under the gallery gives a date of 1833 for the brick nave, with the chancel being added in 1877.

The entrance is through an embattlemented square brick porch of some size. Immediately opposite the door is the original font of the old church, fairly recently rediscovered and behind it, the War Memorial with four attendant British Legion standards. On your left-hand side are the fairly basic 'free pews' with the organ gallery above. The gallery has a bowed-shaped front and balusters, in the centre of which, is a fine carved example of the Royal Coat of Arms of William IV. On your right,

there are box pews of much superior quality, with two five-branch candelabra at the very front. The attention given to every piece of brass-work in this church, from the impressive lectern to the tiniest hinges on the pew doors, is indicative of great devotion.

During the 20th century the church obviously received some notable gifts from benefactors... the beautifully carved wooden pulpit [1935] from the Singer family of sewing machine fame, and before that, gifts from the Baring family [the bankers], who lived at Norman Court. In 1906 they gave the chancel screen with gold painted wrought iron gates and a cross above, and later in 1927, the Riddel Posts, Dossal and Ornaments surrounding the altar. Two very fine 20th century stained glass windows in the north nave wall are both Baring memorials. One is a copy of a window in the church of San Spirito, Florence, and the other a copy of a painting by Fra Bartolommeo [1475-1517].

I could not help but admire the little barrel organ at the front of the nave [recently restored], which I suspect could be older than the stated 1837, for the reason that the very wealthy Denys Rolle [Lord of the Manor, who died in 1797] was a known advocate of their provision in churches to aid in worship. This one has I believe, three separate drums with ten hymns on each.

WEYHILL
St. Michael and All Angels

Gives not the hawthorn bush a sweeter shade to shepherds, looking on their silly sheep, than doth a rich embroidered canopy to kings, that fear their subjects' treachery?
Henry VI. WILLIAM SHAKESPEARE 1564 - 1616

Though shepherds no longer drive their sheep to Weyhill Fair, no doubt during the seven hundred years of its existence, many would have agreed with the words above. The Fair was stipulated to last for three days either side of Michaelmas, and not only were the sheep bought and sold for the London market, but merchants of every conceivable product could be found there. William Langland who wrote the epic poem 'Piers Plowman' in about the year 1362, is thought to have used some of his own experiences at this very fair, when he writes,...

Barones and burgeis and bondmen als[o]
I seigh in the assemble[y], as ye shud here after,
Baxteres[bakers] and brewesteres and bocheres [butchers] manye,
Wolle websteres and weveres of linnen.
Taillours and tinkeres and tolleres in marketes [market toll gatherers]
Masons and minours [miners] and many other craftes.

The Domesday Book records a church here and the interesting presence of a Saxon tomb lid, now built into the exterior wall of the vestry, seems to confirm this.

From the exterior, the church gives the impression of being all of one period, namely Victorian, but in fact the extensive and careful reconstruction of 1863, left the 13th century chancel more or less intact within the new flint and brick exterior. A new pyramid-shaped bellcote once sat like a hat on the roof of the nave until 1907, when Dr. William Smith gave the elegant one we see today, together with its four bells and the clock, in memory of his wife Rachel.

Inside, the south aisle is almost a private chantry chapel of the Gawler family of Ramridge House, and their relations the Smiths. All the windows and wall memorials and perhaps the lectern too, being their several gifts during the last hundred years. High above the Bevington organ, on the wall under the bell tower are two hatchments, [of the Gawler and Loxton families]. The north transept was originally built as a vestry room in 1827; later it was the village school-room, and only in 1863 became integral with the nave. Within it are many memorials, which presumably once graced the south wall of the nave.

On the day of our visit the winter sunshine filtering through the two little lancet windows of the chancel, added to the peace and calm that was indeed centuries old, and in the sanctuary we noticed a carved reredos which looked equally ancient, painted with Christian symbols... the Cross, a fig tree, a vine and lillies, etc.

WHERWELL
St. Peter and Holy Cross

*Through all, a river, like a stream of haze, drew its slow length
until 't was lost in woods.*

ALEXANDER SMITH 1830 - 1867

This is a village, whose history is inextricably linked with the history of its former abbey and that of the monastery of St. Peter in Winchester... perhaps the church's dedication to St. Peter reflects this, and its joint dedication to 'Holy Cross' must surely be the result of the foundation of the adjacent Abbey of Holy Cross, in the year 986 by Elfrida, wife of King Edgar. Her motivation was probably connected with her association with two murders... that of her first husband by her second in Harewood Forest, and that of her husband's successor [her step-son], so that her own son Ethelred could succeed to the throne. The full story is recorded in several places, notably in the guidebook available in the present church, and the 19th century researches of Rev'd. R. H. Clutterbuck, who also stated... 'Wherwell Abbey was the home or the quiet resting place of at least three, and possibly four, English Queens, who were renowned for their extraordinary beauty'.

Elfrida died at Wherwell in 1002; her daughter-in-law Emma, wife of both Ethelred and later, King Canute, was herself forced to reside here in 1043 by her own son, Edward the Confessor. Again in 1051 it was he, who sent his own wife Queen Edith [Eadgyth] here, when her father, Earl Godwin, and his sons were temporarily banished from the kingdom. Just under one hundred years afterwards, both Wherwell, Andover and to a much greater extent Winchester, were scenes of conflict during the wars between King Stephen and his aunt, the Empress Matilda. An engagement between the opposing forces in Wherwell, resulted in both the church and abbey being substantially damaged. Both were rebuilt; the Abbey florishing until its Dissolution on 21st, November 1540. A recent resistivity survey between the neighbouring house, [Wherwell Priory] and the church, has identified the ground-plan of an abbey similar in size to Romsey Abbey... it is amazing to think that such a building could just disappear.

The village church survived, and a print shows that it had a nave and south aisle of almost equal size, quite different to today's building, which is dated 1856. However, what the Victorians built is artistic, neat and appropriate to its setting, inside the most striking new feature is probably the Millennium window by Tony Gillam on the south side. It is a beautiful engraving of 'The Tree of Life' accompanied by village scenes and flowers, linked by a river. In the north-west corner lies the stone effigy of the Abbess Euphemia of 1226, and near by is the 1551 tomb of Sir Owen West, brother of of Sir Thomas, who had obtained the Abbey and its lands from Henry VIII after its dissolution.

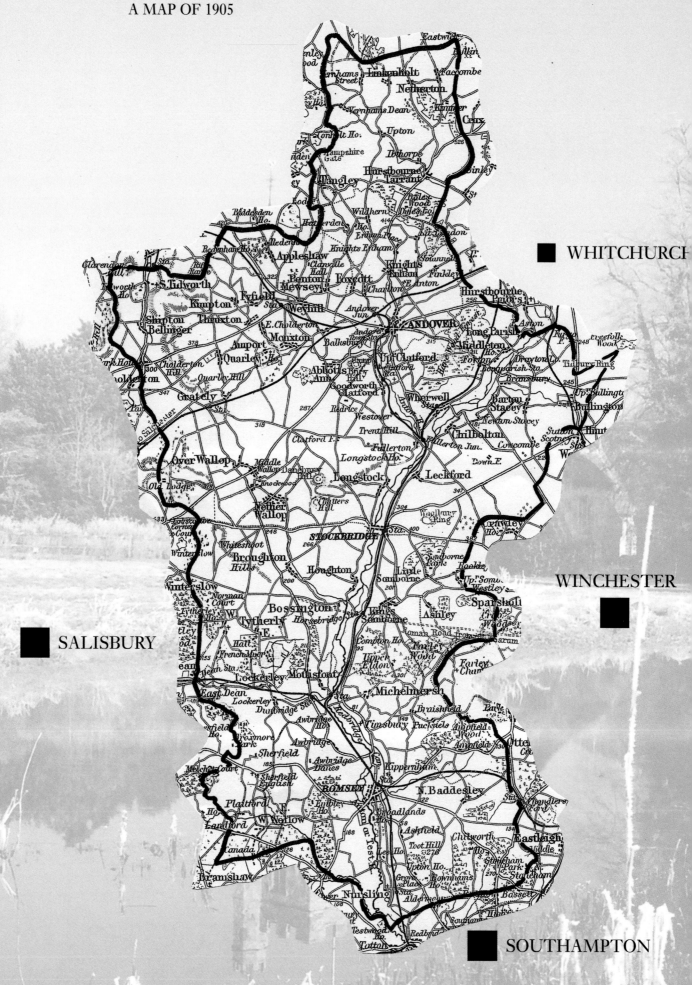

THE TEST VALLEY BOROUGH BOUNDARY
SUPERIMPOSED UPON
A MAP OF 1905

■ WHITCHURCH

■ WINCHESTER

■ SALISBURY

■ SOUTHAMPTON